High School Heroes

 • First Edition 2009 • Manufactured in the United States of America. • All inquiries and permission requests should be addressed to the Publisher, The University of Akron Press, Akron, Ohio 44325-1703.

13 12 11 10 09 5 4 3 2 1

LIBRARY OF CONGRESS CATALOGING-IN-PUBLICATION DATA

Morgan, David Lee.

High school heroes: stories of inspiration, dedication and hope / David Lee Morgan, Jr. — 1st ed.

p. cm. —

ISBN 978-1-931968-66-9 (pbk.: alk. paper)

1. High school athletes—Ohio—Anecdotes. 2. College athletes—Ohio—Anecdotes. 3. School sports—Ohio—Anecdotes. I. Title.

GV346.M67 2009

796.04209771—DC22

2009028388

The paper used in this publication meets the minimum requirements of American National Standard for Information Sciences—Permanence of Paper for Printed Library Materials, ANSI Z39.48–1984. ∞

Articles reprinted with permission of the *Akron Beacon Journal* and Ohio.com.

Cover designed by James Ingram. Images from istockphoto.

The interior was designed and typeset by Amy Freels, with help from Amanda Gilliland. The type was set in Stone Print, with Collegiate display. The interior illustrations are by Amanda Gilliland. The book was printed and bound by BookMasters of Ashland, Ohio.

HIGH SCHOOL HEROES

Stories of Inspiration, Dedication, and Hope

David Lee Morgan Jr.

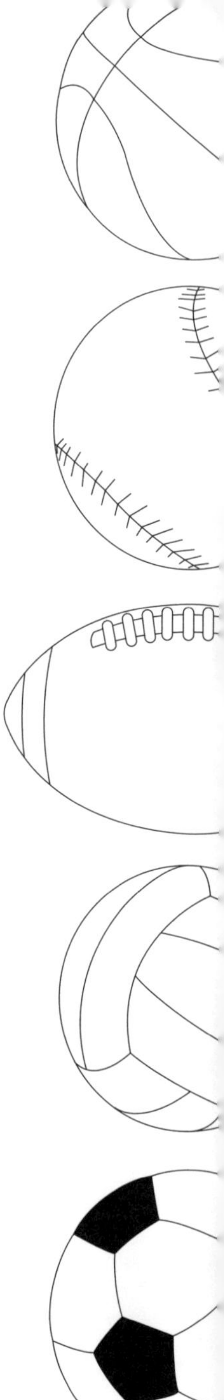

Ringtaw Books • Akron, Ohio

CONTENTS

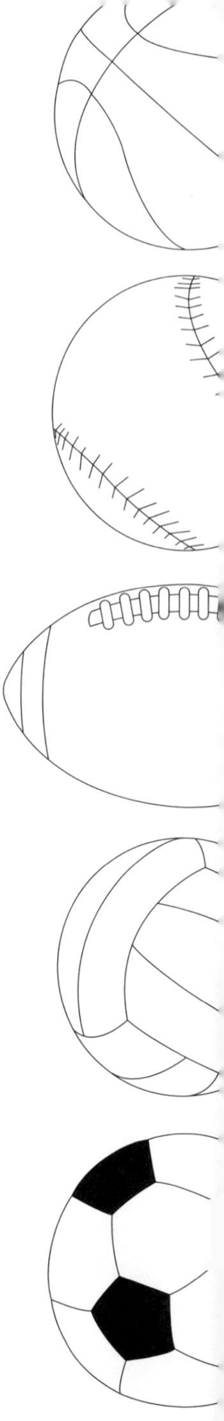

ACKNOWLEDGEMENTS

I'd like to thank the *Akron Beacon Journal* and Tom Bacher of the University of Akron Press for their support and making this project possible.

To my family, wife Tricia, sons Trey and Christian, and daughters Brooke and Cameron (and our dog Vinnie), thanks for all of your support.

And to all of the high school student-athletes in this book, and for those athletes who aren't, know that you are all inspirations to someone, you just don't know it.

FOREWORD

One of the things that I enjoyed most about my years in high school, especially at Glenville High in Cleveland, was the fact that I got a chance to experience so many things that later helped shape me as a man. Playing football for Coach Ted Ginn Sr., one of the most influential and caring men I've ever met (Coach Jim Tressel is the other), I learned that much responsibility came with being a student-athlete and to never take my athletic ability for granted.

I went on to have a lot of success during my college career at The Ohio State University and I was blessed enough to win the Heisman Trophy in 2006. But I couldn't have won that award had it not been for my teammates, Coach Tressel and the entire Ohio State coaching staff and program. The fans meant a lot to me, too. I grew as an athlete, a student and a man during my years at Ohio State and even though we had a lot of success there, my high school years are just as special.

I'm very grateful for my opportunity now to be a quarterback in the NFL and I am unbelievably blessed to have this opportunity. But what's so ironic is the fact that I'm surrounded by the best football players in the world every day. I play against the best football players in the world every Sunday. And sure, there are many of them who have gone on to win Super Bowls, guys who have been All-Pros and guys who have been inducted into the Pro Football Hall of Fame. But no matter how much fame and fortune they experience as professionals, they will never forget the fun and excitement they had during their high school careers, and neither will I.

So if you remember just one thing, remember this: Your high school years will go by faster than you think. Try to cherish each moment on the field or in the classroom. Try to cherish every friendship that you develop, whether it's with a teammate, a classmate, a teacher, your guidance counselor or your principal. Try to get the most out of your entire high school experience as possible because it should be one of the most exciting times of your lives.

So good luck to all of you and here's hoping that you all become "High School Heroes" in one way or another.

Troy Smith, former Ohio State quarterback, 2006 Heisman Trophy winner, and member of the Baltimore Ravens

INTRODUCTION

As a journalist for more than 20 years, I've had the honor and privilege to do many things in this profession, from covering Major League Baseball, the NFL, NBA and several major college programs. But I can honestly say that the biggest enjoyment, the most satisfaction I get from my job is covering high school sports.

I say this with the utmost humility but I feel that the reason why I was named the Ohio Prep Writers Association Writer of the Year three times (2004, 2007 and 2009) is because the sincerity and passion I have for high school sports comes out in the stories I write.

There are so many fascinating stories hidden and tucked away in the hearts, minds and souls of the high school student-athlete that are ready to be told.

Many times, when a student-athlete sees his or her name in the paper, it may be the only time in their lives that they ever get a chance to read about themselves in a positive light in the newspaper.

Once they are in the newspaper, parents and relatives proudly cut out that story and save it for years. Years later, the article is yellow-stained, tattered and torn, but it's still priceless to that family.

That's what I feel about the inspirational high school stories I've written while at the *Akron Beacon Journal* since 1995. Those stories are priceless to me; they are priceless because those young athletes, whatever they accomplished, whatever challenges they faced, they worked hard to overcome their obstacles and become better people.

To me, the collection of columns and feature stories in this book represent the amazing human spirit that young athletes—black, white, male, female, rich or poor, possess. And my hope is that anyone reading this book can look at each individual story and see that these young athletes are inspirations to all of us.

They are all "High School Heroes."

CHAPTER 1

INSPIRATION

Akron Girl's Hard Work Wins Over Neighborhood

Tony Sullivan lives across the street from the tennis courts along Edgewood Avenue near the Akron Zoo. He works on cars his friends bring him to repair. His hands are oil-stained, as are the three wooden chairs outside his home, where he and others often sit and watch one of the area's most amazing stories play out every day.

Firestone junior Christine Coffman, who has qualified for the Division I state tournament this weekend at Ohio State University, walks from her house—a few doors from Sullivan's—to practice at the Edgewood tennis courts. Before long, Sullivan hears her grunts and the squeaks from her sneakers. He knows Coffman is working hard—and doing the neighborhood proud.

Coffman is 17; Sullivan is 54.

Coffman is white; Sullivan is black.

You might think they have nothing in common, but they do. Coffman and Sullivan don't care about age, race, color, gender or socioeconomics. It's all about the human spirit and the simple fact that one person (Sullivan) and one neighborhood (Edgewood) want to see one of their own (Coffman) do well.

There probably are residents along Edgewood who have no idea who Coffman is, or if they happen to see her playing on the courts, think she is a transplant—someone from another side of town using the courts because many are often open there.

Not so. Coffman, an honor student, isn't a transplant. She's a native Edgewood resident, the youngest of six children in Patricia and Donald Coffman's home. Patricia said she couldn't put into words what Christine's diligence and hard work have meant to the family. At the same time, the Coffmans appreciate how people in the community, like Sullivan, support their daughter.

"We're just so proud of Christine because she did this all on her own," Donald said. Coffman said she wouldn't want to practice anywhere else. "I love practicing here," she said. "The tennis courts are right here in my neighborhood and my neighbors are so nice to me. Everybody here knows me and they want my autograph before I leave and walk down the street to go home."

Yes, Coffman has autograph seekers, but don't take that the wrong way. She isn't full of herself or busy thinking that she's the next big thing in tennis. The autograph seekers are neighborhood folks who simply want the humble Coffman to know they appreciate the hard work she has put in to achieve her goal of playing in college.

"I was walking home one day after practice and a lady from her porch yelled to me, 'I'm going to see you on TV one day,'" Coffman said. "That just made me feel so good. I know that I may bring a joy to people here who watch me, but they give me joy just by always being here watching me and encouraging me all the time."

Living in a predominantly black neighborhood where tennis is probably the last thing residents think about on a daily basis, Coffman never looks at race. Young kids in the neighborhood, whether they are coming home from school or playing in their front yards, are drawn to the tennis courts because of Coffman.

Many times she has been practicing for an upcoming match when a youngster, watching he in awe, has walked up and asked, "Can you teach me how to play?"

Coffman said that's the biggest compliment she could receive.

"I'll always hit with them," she said. "When I was their age and I would walk by here and see someone playing, I always wanted someone to show me how to play."

Coffman shatters the stereotypes and myths about affluence and how it pertains to success in athletics. How many other young athletes like Coffman are out there?

That's why Sullivan is proud of Coffman. He has never played tennis. It was too "above" him (he thought), much like golf. But watching Coffman dedicate herself to tennis every day made Sullivan and others along Edgewood proud of her.

"It's not easy for anybody in this neighborhood," Sullivan said. "It's 90 to 95 percent black here. But she lives in our neighborhood and she's at this tennis court faithfully every day. She loves tennis, point-blank. That's why we always support her and make sure she's OK while she's down here practicing."

Because Sullivan sees Coffman's daily regimen, he's in tune with what is going on with her workouts. One day, he said, he saw something peculiar in Coffman's behavior.

"I got off the bus close to my house the other day, and as I walked to my house and passed the courts, I saw Christine sitting on the benches at the far end of the courts, closer to the zoo," Sullivan said.

"When I saw her, she walked onto the courts without her bag and her gear. She went to that far bench and I knew something was wrong, because she never sits on that bench."

Coffman sat alone, without any equipment. There were no sounds coming from the courts.

"I could tell something was on her mind, so I went and sat down next to her," Sullivan said. "She told me she had recently lost two matches earlier that day and she was disappointed and hurt. So we talked, and I just tried to explain to her that you can't win them all. You just have to keep your head up and concentrate on that state [tournament] thing that is coming up. I told her if she keeps having that desire and determination she has, she's going to be all right."

Bicky Mitchell is another Edgewood resident who helps Sullivan with car repairs and supports Coffman. "I'm very proud of her," Mitchell said. "I come out here every day after I get off work and I watch her play. We're out here for a purpose. We do the best we can to encourage her, and like I tell her, 'You're going to have good days and you're going to have bad days. You're going to win some and you're going to lose some, but you're going to be all right.'

"She's very friendly and always smiling. She basically has the support of the neighborhood, believe it or not."

Coffman's tennis career began several years ago, when she met Dan Jones, who grew up in the Elizabeth Park housing projects. Coffman's coach at Firestone is Craig Sampsel, but she also works with Jones, executive director of Say Yes to Tennis Inc. and a certified tennis professional with the United States Professional Tennis Registry.

Jones received his certification from the Van Der Meer Tennis University on Hilton Head Island, S.C. On Jones' Web site, he explains how and why he started his program:

"One day, two young kids were watching me play tennis. Whenever I went to retrieve a ball, I noticed their gaze. I'm sure they resided in the housing development right next to the courts. That housing development is home to some of the most notorious criminals in our city.

"They peered at me longingly. Their look screamed that they would love to play this game but they had no idea of how to play or any means. There was no community tennis association in the area. Conviction gripped me. I decided right then and there that I would start a community tennis program for kids like these. Kids who could not afford the cost of lessons at a club or even the reduced costs of a public parks program would no longer have to peer at the court from the other side of a fence."

Jones remembers the first time he met Coffman.

"To be honest, she snuck into the program when she was too young," he said. "She was 6. But I told a few people that one of these days I'm going to run into a kid who likes tennis more than I do, and whenever I do, I'm going to teach them totally for free. Christine is the only kid I've ever met that loves tennis more than I do."

It's obvious Jones loves teaching Coffman. He is stern at times, very stern. But he knows Coffman can take it and he knows that it will only help her. "She's down here every day before I even get here and she's running," Jones said. "Then she stays after practice and runs again."

And once Coffman packs her bags and leaves the court after several long, hard hours of practice, she makes the short walk down Edgewood, past Sullivan and his friends, past the old lady, past the young kids playing in their yards and she is proud—proud to live on Edgewood.

AUTHOR'S INSPIRATION

The "Author's Inspiration" for this book came from Christine. Her dedication and commitment to the sport amazed me. What amazed me even more was the fact that Coffman's story reached across race and class. It was a story that came along at a time in our country when tensions were high because of the economic, political and even racial climate. Christine showed that there are so many good people, so many good neighborhoods and so many good neighbors that are doing the right thing. The same holds true for high school student-athletes.

Christine's story was inspirational enough, but the 30-plus emails I received from this story were the most I had EVER received in my career, and they were all positive. I thought I'd share a few:

- My wife and I wanted to write you to tell you how much we appreciated and enjoyed your article on the young lady from Edgewood Ave. What a pleasure to read a positive, heartwarming story in these times of negativity and nasty politics. Your article was very well written and showed the positive side of living in a "mixed" neighborhood and how supportive we can all be of one another if we would just get past "surface issues." She is a winner in our book.

- I read with great pleasure the article you wrote last week regarding Firestone tennis player Christine Coffman. With all the "stuff" that goes on with pro and college athletes it is left to the high school athletes (most of them anyway) to give us the true meaning of competition and the human spirit. Beyond that, it was even more touching and heartwarming about how her local neighborhood community "adopted" her and shared in her success.
- I can't say enough about the wonderful story you wrote about Chrissy and the neighborhood. I was deeply moved by your sensitivity to her, her supporters and the neighborhood in general.
- At the State Tournament the coach from Canton Hoover approached me and had nothing but great things to say about your article and Chrissy. He said, "I admire her so much because she is doing this the old fashioned way. Just a bunch of hard work with little money supporting her." He went on the mention how rare it is these days to see a kid perform at her level who is from a public school.

Just as a follow up about the tournament. The girl who was the eventual winner, Kerra Sherwood, is the girl who beat Chrissy in that grueling 3 set match at the Districts in Oberlin. It just goes to show how close Chrissy is to the top players in Ohio. Finally, it was such an honor to have our program, Chrissy and the neighborhood mentioned in our hometown newspaper. I spoke with Tony Sullivan yesterday. Can you believe he told me that he and some of the old guys in the 'hood are collecting some money to try to help with her training and tournament costs?

A Warrior of All Seasons, Senior Fitz Green's High Energy Belies Family Grief

I met Walsh Jesuit senior defensive back/special teams player Fitz Green on Tuesday. This incredible young man, whose full name is Ryan Fitzgerald Green, caught my eye Saturday, when the Warriors came from behind to beat Chagrin Falls 21–17 in a Division III regional semifinal game.

Walsh's Armand Dehaney, Kyle Snyder and Cameron Ontko made most of the big plays, but Green was doing a lot of the grunt work. Early in the game Green almost blocked a punt. Seconds later, he was at the other end making a block on the return. He also comes in on certain defensive schemes as an extra linebacker and covers punts.

It seemed like wherever the ball was, Green was. He wasn't Walsh's leading tackler. He's not close to being the biggest player on the team at 5-foot-11, 165 pounds, but his energy was mesmerizing. You would never know by watching Green on the football field that he has seen his share of heartbreak and pain in the past few years.

When Green was a sophomore, he saw his mother succumb to a long battle with cancer. Sue Green was 41 and left behind Fitz, along with his sister, Halley, who was 14 at the time, and younger brother, Jack, who was 9.

You hear the word "courageous" used a lot when someone talks about a cancer victim. It's because it takes the courage of 1,000 lions to come face to face with the realization that this horrendous, vile disease eventually will claim your life. So for those like Sue, they are courageous.

Then, this past weekend, Green's aunt passed away.

"To be honest, at first, it's hard to understand the 'whys'—you know, 'Why is this happening to me?'" said Green, one of the most well-respected and liked players on the team. "But it has helped me gain perspective on things. It helped me realize all the wonderful things I've been given in life."

The gridiron is where Green leaves behind all the grief the world has brought to his feet for a few hours and he joins his football brothers in an escapade of bruising, bone-crushing, teeth-chattering fun. "It's something I get excited about," Green said. "Being a senior and being in the playoffs, I know every game might be my last, so I go out and make the best of it."

Gerry Rardin, who is in his 29th season as the Warriors' coach, said Green could be a role model to student-athletes everywhere. "Fitz's attitude and effort never falters," said Rardin, whose 9–2 team faces Aurora (10–2) in the regional final Saturday night at Solon. "It's most important for high school kids to realize that everyone isn't going to be a starter, but they are still just as important as the star player."

The respect Green has from his teammates is obvious and admirable. As I walked to the locker room after practice to interview Green, Snyder and Dehaney were sitting on a huge rock, banging mud from their spikes. When I greeted them and told them I was there to talk to Green, their eyes lit up. They were excited and proud.

"That is great," said Dehaney, a Ball State recruit. "He plays his heart out every time he's out on the field. He's a great guy and a great teammate."

Snyder, who is deciding where he'll play next year from among several options, said he and Dehaney have a nickname to honor Green.

"We call him the 'Unsung Warrior,'" Snyder said. "That's actually an award the team gives out every year, and when we think of that award, we think of that young man. Fitz doesn't get the press clippings that some of the other guys on the team get, but he exemplifies everything that a Walsh football player is supposed to exemplify. With everything that he's gone through, he shows how strong he is by coming to practice day in and day out with a great attitude, and he gets it done."

For Green, his teammates are like brothers.

"I love these guys, so when we lose, I feel so terrible for everyone," he said. "And when we win, I feel great because it's a great sense of accomplishment as a team. I love these guys and the coaching staff. It's an amazing family. So now, when I play football or do anything, I'm doing it just to make my mom proud. When my mom died, it put so many things in perspective. I don't get worked up, because after seeing what my mom went through, there are bigger things in life than football. I mean, I want to play football in college if I can, because it's a great thing. But it's not the only thing."

As Green fondly talked about his mother, I asked a question I knew would warm his heart.

"Was your mom a good cook?"

He smiled, and with an all-American kid look, replied, "She was a great cook. Her beef stroganoff was amazing and I loved walking into the house and smelling it if we were having it for dinner. And she made the best chocolate chip cookies, too."

After the interview was over, I shook Green's hand as he walked into the locker room to put in his mandatory 30 minutes of post-practice weightlifting.

And as I packed my notebook and watched Green disappear, all I could think about was what that young man would give for a hot plate of his mom's beef stroganoff and warm and chewy chocolate chip cookies.

AUTHOR'S INSPIRATION

Fitz was one of those young men who stood out to me because of his energy and passion on the field. He wasn't a full-time starter, but when he did start or when he was called upon, he never gave less than 110 percent. I covered one particular game where I watched Fitz for several minutes. He made tackles, patted his teammates on the back after a great play, extended his hand to help an opposing player off the ground after a tackle and he was just a gentleman on the field.

I decided I wanted to meet this young man and possibly write a feature about him. When I told coach Gerry Rardin, he couldn't have been happier; Fitz was one of the nicest and hard-working players he had ever coached. And Rardin said a feature on Fitz would do the young man a world of good because he had lost his mother to cancer and later, lost an aunt to illness. So he had gone through some tough times, but all the while, he kept plugging away in his mom and aunt's memory. To me, Fitz will always be a "High School Hero."

All Players Have Shot to Live Dream: But While Some Wait They Contribute From Sideline

While listening to one of my favorite songs in my car Thursday afternoon, moments after talking to a man who thanked me for mentioning his son in a column I wrote in the fall, this occurred to me—every high school sports team needs more cowbell.

More cowbell? Yes—I'll explain.

During this past football season, I wrote about a freshman football player at a local high school who rarely played in freshman games, let alone varsity games.

"Jimmy" wasn't big, or fast or strong. But he loved nothing more than being on that football field on Friday nights dressing as a varsity player. You couldn't have found a more inspiring kid, which is why I mentioned him in my column.

Jimmy was passionate about his school, his teammates and the fact that he had even been given the opportunity to stand on the same sideline with all of those senior and junior starters.

For Jimmy, it was a privilege he didn't take lightly. On the sideline, he was a cheerleader in a football uniform—and I mean that with the utmost respect.

By now, you're asking yourself, "what the heck does all of this have to do with a cowbell?"

Plenty.

Jimmy's story is the same story in every sport, at every school, every year. I've seen the same thing during basketball season this year—a marginal player dreaming about how he or she has the ball, with the clock winding down. They take that final shot at the buzzer and it hits nothing but net. The crowd goes crazy and the star player is carried off the court riding the shoulders of delirious fans.

But in reality, that player is sitting at the end of the bench, or standing on the sidelines thinking, "I hope coach puts me in so I can show him/her what I can do. I know I can do it."

These are players who aren't stars and sometimes feel no one cares about them or the effort they give every day in practice, when the cameras and reporters aren't there.

The fact is, these kids take pride in their roles on the scout team, or as glorified cheerleaders on the bench. They just want to be part of a team and at the conclusion of the season, whether they lost every game, won a championship or accomplished something in between, their satisfaction is that they were part of a team.

(Here comes the music connection).

So I'm listening to Steely Dan, and there's one particular song I like because of the subtle but extremely effective Hammond organ that's being played in the background, which enhances the song and gives it that full, soulful, Gospel-like sound. Subtle but effective.

In another song, it's the drummer, lightly tapping on the high-hat, with a steady rhythm during the entire track who makes the song unique. You have to really listen closely to hear and appreciate the sound.

In yet another song, it's the bass player fingering the same basic riff over and over that holds the song together and gives it that "Wow!"

Which leads me to the cowbell.

One of my favorite *Saturday Night Live* skits of all time is the one when cast members, including Will Ferrell on cowbell, spoofed the rock band Blue Oyster Cult. Veteran actor Christopher Walken played famed music producer and Grammy Award-winning Bruce Dickinson.

The band was in studio trying to make a triumphant comeback and playing a track for Dickinson that starts out sounding really good. Then, Ferrell, standing in the background, as if he is a scout team member, begins to passionately play the cowbell, loud, strong and proud.

The band members thought it was ruining the song and stopped playing abruptly.

Ferrell's character, Gene Frenkle says, "I'll be doing myself a disservice . . . and every member in this band, if I don't perform the hell out of this." Ferrell, or should I say Frenkle, is like all of those scout team players, who feel that they would be doing their teammates, school and community a disservice if they didn't play their butts off in practice, and in a game, if they ever got the chance.

Meanwhile, Walken's character, Dickinson, delivers this classic and hilarious line to Ferrell (Frenkle), "Guess what? I got a fever! And the only prescription . . . is MORE COWBELL!"

Every high school team needs a Dickinson, who understands the importance of a Frenkle. Every high school team needs more cowbell.

AUTHOR'S INSPIRATION

Adam Hamad was the inspiration for this column. I was covering a football game at his high school—Akron Archbishop Hoban—and I couldn't help noticing this young man. Not because of his imposing size. In fact, the irony is that he was so noticeable because of his diminutive size—he was 4-foot-10, 100-pounds as a freshman. His heart and spirit were three times bigger.

He was one of the hardest workers on the team, the biggest cheerleader on the sideline and never complained about any lack of playing time. Adam played for the Knights for four years and gave every ounce to that program. To those who don't know Adam, you could form the conclusion that he was just one of those players who was just "on the team." He was more than that. He epitomized what it means to be a team player, whether you were a starter, a backup a team manager or even the water boy or girl. He was respected by his teammates and the coaching staff because of his dedication to the program and he's a better person because of that experience. He was *Rudy*.

Hudson Wins Girls Team Title: Walsh Jesuit a Close Second as Copley Endures Baton Drop During Exchange

Sometimes a great sports story isn't always about who wins. Sometimes a great story emerges from adversity and disappointment. In the Division I boys and girls district track meet Friday at Ravenna, three stories stood out.

First was Hudson and Walsh Jesuit battling it out for the girls title. Hudson, who had district champs in the long jump (Rachel Dahlby), 1,600-meter-race (Kate Tejkl) and 400 relay (Dahlby, Sarah Wilke, Catherine White and Elyse Adams) won the team title with 125 points. Walsh was second with 109 points.

The top four individuals and teams in each event advance to the regional meet next week in Austintown.

"We've been stepping up every week, and we've worked really hard for this," Hudson coach Paul Milligan said of winning the school's fourth-consecutive district title.

In the boys competition, Solon (108) held off Copley (107) to win the championship.

But there was a third story in the meet, which helped put sports in perspective and could serve as a life lesson for all high school student-athletes.

It was the story of Copley's 400 relay team, which consists of senior Carrie Dyer, sophomore Reonee Dunn, sophomore Desire Greer and senior Jennifer Legrair.

The team entered the finals as one of the favorites. But Dunn, who runs the second leg, and Greer who runs the third leg, had a little trouble with their exchange, and the baton was dropped. The Indians never recovered and finished last.

Dunn was devastated as she watched Legrair try to make up ground in the last leg. But when Dunn saw that Legrair had finished last, Dunn collapsed to the turf in tears. She stayed there for several minutes until Dyer sprinted from near the finish line to the other end of the field—where Dunn was—to console her. Dyer lifted Dunn's head from the turf, then gave her a hug.

Dyer and Legrair could have pointed fingers, especially considering that this was the last time they had the chance to run that event. But the two knew friendship was more important.

"I didn't want Reonee to feel bad because I could have tripped and fell flat on my face at the start," said Dyer, who will play basketball at Wittenberg University. "I just asked her if she tried her best and did everything she could do. She said yes, and that's all you can ask."

Legrair said: "She kept saying she was sorry over and over, and I just told her that no one was mad at her."

Moments later, members of the Copley boys 400 relay team, which finished third, made their way over to Dunn to console her, even though the team had to get ready for its race.

"We feel really bad for Reonee," said sophomore sprinter Tre' Legrair. "We just had to go over and show her that we support her." Then the rest of the girls team surrounded Dunn and gave her a group hug.

"I feel really bad, but when my teammates came over to me, I knew they all still loved me," Dunn said, as she started crying tears of happiness. "We're going to come back and do better next year. And every time I run this event next year and the year after that, I'll always be thinking about Carrie and Jen."

AUTHOR'S INSPIRATION

I never saw an athlete take a disappointment as hard as Reonee Dunn. This Copley girls relay team was going to state, no question. All the team had to do was get on the track, do its thing and it was off to Columbus. Well, Reonee made an unintentional mistake of dropping the baton and Copley failed to advance to the state meet.

Reonee was devastated and was slumped on the infield crying uncontrollably. I felt so bad for her because I knew exactly how she felt. She felt like she had let the team down. She didn't want to get up or face anyone because she was disgraced.

She should have never felt that way because we all make mistakes and we become better people by learning from our mistakes. To me, the great story was how all of her teammates—girls and boys on the Copley track team—came to her side to let her know that it was OK and that making it to state wasn't nearly as important as showing Reonee how much they cared and loved her and didn't want to see her hurting so badly.

Parker Slam Dunks Basketball, Myths: Her Win in National Event Brings Credibility to Girls Game, Hope to Players

Fellas.

C'mon now. Don't playa hate.

Give Candace Parker her due. The 6-foot-3, Naperville, Ill., high school senior, who is a two-time Naismith Award winner, won the Powerade Jam Fest as part of the McDonald's All-American High School Team competition Monday in Oklahoma City.

Parker, a Tennessee Lady Vols recruit, became the first girl to win the Slam Dunk contest. LeBron James won the contest last year.

I'm sure some of you guys are trying to figure out how in the world a "girl" could outdunk some of the nation's top male high school players. It's like trying to figure why Krzyzewski is pronounced sha-chef-ski.

I know when you think of spectacular dunks, you think of James flying through the air, with a defender standing underneath the basket trying to take a charge, only to see LeBron add to his *SportsCenter* Top 10 Highlight resume.

Or you're used to seeing Toronto's Vince Carter throwing down a dunk that electrifies a crowd.

In truth, Parker's dunks weren't very impressive.

OK, she did come up with a creative idea which helped her receive perfect scores of 10 from the judges. As Parker took off for the basket, she covered her face briefly with her arm, as if she were going to dunk without looking, but during the last few steps, she removed her arm from her face and threw the ball down.

Naturally, Parker didn't have the same hang time as her male counterparts and she didn't deliver the dunk with the same authority and intensity.

But she completed her three dunks.

Some of the other competitors didn't, and the most important rule in the contest is that you must complete three dunks. You have to credit the other guys, however, for not trying to be too conservative so that they didn't lose to a girl. After seeing that Parker had completed her dunks, the guys continued to try to impress the crowd and the television audience.

Let's not kid ourselves, though. If you went out to the streets and had a slam dunk contest, Parker would not have had a chance. But in this particular case, Parker got the job done, plain and simple.

And forget about the silly notion that the judges wanted to see a girl win, or that she used a women's-sized ball, which gave her an advantage. Those arguments are ridiculous.

Just for one minute, look at the accomplishment objectively and understand the importance of Parker winning the contest.

"I was pretty surprised that she won and I'm happy," said Hoban girls head basketball coach Jacki Windon, a former point guard at Hoban and Gannon University. "I think (Parker) winning may show people that women who play basketball are becoming more athletic and that the game is starting to evolve even more."

Think about some of the young women across the country who play basketball and are passionate about the game just as much as boys.

When my 9-year-old daughter Brooke saw Parker's dunk on *Sports-Center*, she couldn't believe her eyes. She jumped off the couch and said, "Dad, is that really a girl? I can't believe it. Man, that's awesome."

Next thing you know, Brooke is bouncing off the couch trying to imitate Parker's dunk.

Parker sparked something—hope—in my daughter much like the WNBA did for other aspiring young ladies who love the game of basketball.

Congratulations Candace. And you go, girl!

AUTHOR'S INSPIRATION

My daughter, Brooke, is a huge basketball fan. Lisa Leslie is and will always be her favorite professional basketball player. One day, while I was watching *SportsCenter*, I saw that Candace Parker, who went on to have a magnificent career at the University of Tennessee and also was a member of the United State's Gold Medal winning team in the 2008 Beijing Olympics, won the McDonald's All-American Slam Dunk contest. Yes the slam dunk contest that LeBron James won several years before as a high school senior.

When Brooke saw the news, she couldn't believe it. She even asked me, "Dad, is that true? Is that for real?" I answered, "Yep, honey." Brooke's eyes were as wide as saucers and I could tell her heart just swelled with pride. She was so proud of Parker's accomplishment—becoming the first female to win the event. I had never seen my daughter that proud of someone she had never met before but it told me how much it meant to Brooke, and probably so many other young women.

Girl Becomes Gridiron Star: Mogadore Coach Says Quarterback Is Big Part of Peewee Team's Success 'She Hits Them Right Back'

And the quarterback wore a pink dress to the team's party. Of course, heads turned. But not for the reasons you may think.

Rather, it was because Jordan Michelle Poth—she with the sandy-blond hair and an ever-present twinkle in her eyes—just looked so darn cute.

The 12-year-old is a varsity starter on a Mogadore Wildcats peewee (tackle) football team. The team—which is 5–1—gives a lion's share of the credit for its last two victories to Jordan's throwing and running prowess.

"We don't miss a beat with her," said Tom Rosato, Jordan's coach and an 18-year veteran of coaching. "And she's as accurate as any of them. She runs offense just as good as anyone we have.

"I have a lot of confidence in her," he continued. "So does the entire team. In fact, these kids treat her no differently than any of the other boys. That's what I'm most proud of. They hit her as hard as they do anyone else, and she hits them right back."

Jordan has been playing football since she was 7. She played running back and defensive positions before this season. Some might say she's a natural for the game, and the varsity quarterback position in particular.

Jordan's father, Steve Poth, was a stellar starting quarterback for Mogadore High School and Kent State University. Her older brother played quarterback for Springfield High School. So, what was Jordan—the only girl in a family that includes four brothers—to do but get in the game?

In fact, the 5-foot-1-inch girl who is all of 100 pounds is in every game you can imagine: basketball and fast-pitch softball, as well as football. In fact, she's on the Ohio Lightning, a traveling youth softball team.

"I told Jordan she could do what she wanted (about playing football)," Steve Poth said. "She's always liked football. It's her favorite sport. And I found out she always wanted to play football."

Quiet and unassuming off the field, Jordan proves Saturday after Saturday she has the moxie to get things done once she's in her No. 12 green-and-white jersey.

Well, consider the team's winning record. "We lost to Ellet, six to nothing in the first game of the season," Rosato volunteered. "But we came back. We won our last two games 8–6 because of Jordan." Brian Moore, who attends most of Jordan's games, is just as effusive with praise for his goddaughter's grace under pressure on the football field. "Just to think, I bought her first walker," he says, journeying back.

Bill Rosato Sr., a head coach in the nine-team Mogadore peewee league, has inspired three of his sons and his grandson to get involved. He has been coaching for more than 41 years. He even coached Steve Poth and his brother, Mike.

You'd think at 72, the elder Rosato would be something of a dinosaur when it comes to girls in the game. Nothing could be further from the truth, he insisted, as long as they can play.

"Jordan's won five games; so she's got to be doing something right!" the elder Rosato said. "I've got to give her credit. But I do worry about her getting hurt," he said.

Jordan, who speaks softly and with an economy of words, doesn't fret in that regard.

"I've got a good line," she shrugged, referring to her teammates.

Asked how long she plans to stay in the game of football, Jordan has a short answer: "We'll see."

So, being heir apparent to her father's high school or college quarterback jobs isn't even in her vocabulary. Incidentally, her father, uncle and grandfather, Joe Poth, all coach in the Mogadore peewee league.

The Wildcats—no strangers to female teammates—had Brooke Roepkin as a kicker last year. She's now kicking for Mogadore High School's freshman team.

Cassie Poth—Jordan's mother—said football will help bolster her daughter's character. "I tell her to be confident and tough," Cassie Poth said. "It's a good, good way to build up her self-esteem. That way she'll have a better chance of saying 'no' to other things down the road." Her daughter also has the legs for shopping. "I drop long before she does," Cassie Poth marvels. "She also has quite a shoe fetish." Something tells me she wasn't talking about cleats.

It's not a secret in Mogadore that Jordan Poth is a star quarterback for the Wildcats' youth football team, even though she's a female.

"When we're playing against teams that don't know I'm a girl, they don't say anything," said Jordan, an eighth-grader at Mogadore Middle School. "But when they find out, they're surprised.

"I just want to show them that I don't stink as a player."

Poth, who can take the snap from center, drop back and throw spirals 15 and 20 yards downfield with pin-point accuracy, has led her team to a national youth football tournament to be played later this week in Daytona Beach, Fla.

"Jordan does a great job for us and she just goes out there and makes plays," coach Thom Rosato said. "We have so much confidence in what she can do. She's just a thrill to watch." The Wildcats won the Suburban Youth Football Association's age 12–14 championship with a 9–1 record.

Thanks to fund-raising efforts, the team chartered two buses and departed Monday for Florida. The Wildcats play on Thanksgiving Day and Saturday against teams from Massachusetts and Georgia.

Coach Bill Rosato Sr., who has been coaching youth football for 44 years, said: "She just lets her playing on the field do all the talking. She's the best quarterback we've ever had, and we've had some good ones."

Jordan's dad, Steve Poth, was a standout quarterback for Mogadore in the 1980s and later played at Kent State. One of Jordan's four brothers, Joe, was a three-year player at Mogadore before finishing his senior year as quarterback at Springfield.

"Jordan has been playing football since she was 3," Joe Poth said. "She would always be out there with me and my brothers throwing the football around and she's really developed into a good player. I'm proud of her."

Jordan added: "I love to play all sports but I really like football. These guys are like brothers to me and they have all made me feel comfortable because we just want to play football and win. Nobody on the team cares that I'm a girl."

Tom Rosato enjoys seeing fans marvel at Jordan's athleticism. "I was at home one day watching a videotape of one of our games," he said. "Jordan threw a long touchdown pass and you could hear one of the coaches on the tape say, 'He's good. That quarterback is really good.' Then, the guy paused and said, 'No. Really? You're kidding me!' That's when he realized Jordan was a girl."

Jordan's teammates say playing with a girl has never been an issue. "We've been playing with Jordan for years and everybody is fine with it," said Zach Glagola, a tight end and cornerback for the Wildcats. "Everyone treats her like she's just one of the guys," said running back Kodey Chance. "But she's a nice girl, and I think she's pretty."

AUTHOR'S INSPIRATION

I received a call from someone in Mogadore about this amazing girl who was the quarterback for a youth football team. I'm always a sucker for a good "girl-playing-football story." So when I arrived at Mogadore High School football field on a cold November evening I was looking for Jordan. I'm not sure exactly what I was looking for, all I know is I knew Jordan was a quarterback and couldn't believe my eyes when I saw the quarterback for this team run a few plays.

Then I walked up to an assistant coach who was expecting me and asked, "Was THAT Jordan?" He proudly answered, with a big smile, "Yep." This girl was awesome. She played the game the right way—regardless of her gender.

Franek Is Absolutely Fantastic

The peanut butter and double chocolate banana split that Crestwood senior Bridget Franek happily scarfed down was the perfect dessert for a perfect afternoon.

During the (2006) girls state track and field championships at Ohio State's Jesse Owens Memorial Stadium last week, Franek did something that had never been done, by a girl or a boy.

Franek won state championships in all three distance events—the 800-, 1,600, and 3,200-meter races and set state records in the 800 (2:11.22) and the 3,200 (10:43.86).

She also was a member of the 3,200-meter relay team, along with junior Cassie Schenck, junior Megan Miller and freshman Nicole Cozzone, that won the state championship. And to top off the day, Crestwood won the Division II overall state championship, the first time in school history.

Later that evening, Franek hung out with her teammates at their hotel room, eating ice cream, relaxing in a hot tub and celebrating the monumental and historic individual and team achievements.

"That day was just so awesome," said Franek, who will run at Penn State next season. "All I wanted to do is hang out with my friends and it was so much fun to just relax and not worry about having to run again."

That's when Franek's tone turned a little somber. "While we were all together, it was really sad, actually, because we knew we wouldn't be running together anymore," she said. "We were excited that we won the state championship but we were also very sad. It was bittersweet."

Penn State coach Beth Sullivan was in Columbus recruiting and watched Franek's performance. "It was cool having (Sullivan) her there," Franek said. "She wasn't there just to watch me, but I'm glad she got to see me do all of that. I know she's probably seen a lot more, especially at the college level, but I was glad she got a chance to see me interact with my friends from the team because they are great."

Meanwhile, Bridget's dad, Tom Franek, went to church the Sunday after the state championship with his son Josh, who will be a sophomore at Crestwood. Bridget's mom, Rosalie, was still in Columbus with her daughter. But Tom said members of St. Ambrose's Parish in Garrettsville were buzzing after reading about Franek's outstanding performance.

"When Josh and I went to church, people had the article with them and everyone was teary-eyed just talking about it," said Tom, who won state championships in cross country and the 3,200 while at Kenston. "I'm still in awe at what she did. And when the fans (14,000-plus) gave her a standing ovation after she won the 3,200, I was in the stands just bawling."

So was Rosalie, who also was an accomplished runner at Midpark. "It was pretty incredible," Rosalie said, as she started to get emotional. "It was a culmination of a lot of hard work. She's a good kid and it was fun to watch her evolve into a runner. She's amazing."

St. Ambrose priest, Father Richard Pentello, had nothing but praise for what Bridget accomplished.

He said that particular Sunday was definitely a joyous occasion.

"We're so proud of Bridget and everyone in the parish knows what a fine person she is," Father Pentello said.

"She's such a good all-around person, she's active in the church, she's an exceptional student and most of all, she's very humble. She doesn't flaunt her talents and it's because she has a great family and (Tom and Rosalie) raised good kids."

Bridget said she got a taste of being somewhat of a local celebrity earlier this week. She was on a run with her mom, when they decided to stop at the local Marc's store to buy some markers for a scrapbook.

"It was so cool," she said excitedly. "One lady recognized me and said, 'You're Bridget Franek, aren't you? Can I bag those for you?' "

Yet, Franek is keeping everything in perspective. "It really hasn't hit me yet," she said, referring to her stellar state championship performance. "I think looking back on my career, I'm pretty happy how it all progressed. Now, I'm ready for college, but I'm going to miss all of my friends and teammates."

AUTHOR'S INSPIRATION

The day I witnessed Bridget make Ohio high school history with her four state championships in one day, I was absolutely blown away, because Bridget blew away her competition all year. But she did it in such a humble and sportsmanship-like way, always congratulating her opponents, always greeting them with a smile, a hug and sincere conversation.

Bridget went on to run at Penn State where, heading into the 2008 season as a junior, she was already the holder of numerous Penn State records. She was the 2007 Penn Relays Steeplechase Champion; 2007 Big Ten Freshman of the Year; ran a school-record 9:59.21 to win the steeplechase at the Penn Relays—the second-fastest time ever run at historic Franklin Field, among other accomplishments. I wouldn't be surprised one bit if I saw Bridget representing our country in the 2012 Olympics. I know she would make all of us proud.

Umping the Ante: West Akron Baseball Gets First Girl Umpire

The voice from behind the umpire's mask was strong and commanding. "FOUL BALL!"

As the inning ended during a recent West Akron Baseball H-League game at Fairlawn Elementary, the umpire's mask came off. Long, dark hair cascaded down around the umpire's shoulders and the face of 14-year-old Sara Miller was revealed to the teams of 9- and 10-year-olds. Sara, who will be a freshman at Firestone High School in the fall, is the only female umpire in the West Akron Baseball league.

"Last year, we had difficulties in H-League with some of the umpires because even though they were teenage boys, you couldn't hear them call balls or strikes," said Fred Carque, who is the coach of the White Sox.

"So this year, when Sara umpired one of our games, my first impression was, 'We have a girl umpiring our game?'" "Well, Sara did a wonderful job," Carque continued. "But what impressed me the most was the way she handled things when I questioned her balls and strike in between innings. She just said, 'Coach, I'm calling them as I see them.' After that, I turned around and thought, 'What more could you ask from an umpire?' "

Sara umpires up to four games a week, if she's working a Saturday doubleheader.

"I started umpiring because I love baseball and grew up around it," Sara said. "My dad coached and umpired and my (two older) brothers all played baseball, so umpiring was something I knew I could do."

"I was afraid of what people would say or if they would approve of me," she added. "At first, they looked at me like just another girl, and I didn't appreciate it. But it's all about knowing what you're doing. You have to take control of the game and show that you're not going to take anything. You still want everybody to have fun, though."

Sara said she's even given thought to sticking with umpiring.

"I want to see where it takes me," she said.

Her father, Tom Miller, has been the league's director of umpires the past four years and is still umpiring youth games when he's not traveling the country as an over-the-road truck driver for Van Baren Cartage Co.

Tom Miller made sure his daughter knew the rules of the game. More importantly, he wanted her to respect the game before she put on the customary mask, chest protector and shin guards.

"She probably has forgotten more about baseball than some boys actually know," Tom Miller said.

The Miller family support for Sara is nonstop.

Kim Miller, Sara's mother, said she couldn't be more proud of her daughter's drive to take on a position males dominate from Little League to professional baseball.

"Sara has been watching baseball since she was a toddler, so when she asked her dad if she could umpire, I knew she could do it," Kim Miller said.

So what does the rest of Sara's family think of her summertime job, which pays $20 a game? "Based on what I've seen, she's more than capable of umpiring boys games, and I'd love to work with her," said Sara's older brother, Michael, a 2003 Firestone graduate who will be a junior at the University of Cincinnati this fall. "She has my utmost confidence, and I'm glad to see that she is doing well."

Sara's other brother, Matt, was a starting junior outfielder last season for the Firestone baseball team, which won the City Series championship. "Sara is very professional because she's been around baseball for so long," Matt Miller said. "All she needs is more experience because she's confident in what she does."

And Sara's little sister, Taylor, 11, has a slightly different take: "It makes me feel good to see her out there with the boys. And if they don't listen to her, she can punch them out."

AUTHOR'S INSPIRATION

A friend asked me to come and watch his son's youth baseball game one summer day. I said, "No problem." Once I got to the field, I greeted my friend and waved to his son, who was out in the field playing my favorite position, second base.

I started watching the game and I couldn't help but notice how professional the umpire was behind the plate. Not to take anything away from the young people who umpire youth baseball in the summer (I did it while in high school for extra money) but they aren't in it for a career. But this umpire seemed to be different.

That was an understatement. At the end of the inning, the umpire took off the mask and this long hair cascaded down.

It was Sara. I knew Sara from the neighborhood but never knew she umpired, and I definitely didn't know that she could umpire that well.

The rest of the game, all I thought about was writing a column about how great of a job she did and that maybe she could be a role model for other young women who loved the game of baseball and were interested in following Sara's footsteps.

Family Affair: Sisters Raise St. V-M Football Player

St. Vincent-St. Mary football player Chris House walked across the artificial turf at Green Street Stadium. It was Senior Night, Week 9 of his final high school season. Two of the three most important people in his life were at his side.

They're three women who love him and who taught him what it means to be a man when their parents couldn't be there to raise him—or even to watch his first organized football game.

The women—sisters—shared Chris' loss when their mother, Betsy House, died of cancer in January 1995 and when the disease claimed their father, Bill, in July 1996. The family's oldest child, Jennifer, then 24, took custody of the siblings, Becky, 16; Maggie, 12; and Chris, 7.

"I would have to say, for a few years, I think I was just on automatic pilot, and all I did was focus on the kids because I didn't have to think about me or how I felt about losing Mom and Dad or anything," said Jennifer, a legal assistant at the law firm of Marshall, Dennehey, Warner, Coleman & Goggin. "As the kids got older and stopped needing me as much, I had a really hard time. It wasn't until several years after my mom and dad died that it all hit me, and I pretty much fell apart. The three of them got together and took care of me for a while."

Jennifer said that when her mom passed away, her dad started getting things in place so that a relative could take care of the family if something happened to him. The unthinkable happened barely a year later.

After being diagnosed with cancer, Bill House was told he didn't have much time to live. Jennifer knew what she had to do: keep her family together. She was attending the University of Akron and had never lived away from her family.

"I told my dad I really wanted to take custody of Chris and the girls," Jennifer said. "He had a really hard time with that because he felt that no parent should leave this kind of responsibility to one of his children. I told him if he didn't, he would make my life worse."

The special bond the siblings had formed grew stronger. "Chris and I were very close when he was younger," said Becky, now 26 and a nurse at Barberton Citizens Hospital. "I took more of the mother role over Chris. I think I still do. I worry about him.

"When I went to Ohio State for two years, I still remember when they dropped me off. Chris was hanging out of the van crying, 'Don't leave! Don't leave!' Chris and I were very, very close."

Maggie chimed in: "Two peas in a pod. Yeah, they would sit on the porch and have late-night talks," Jennifer added, sounding like a proud mother. Chris didn't hesitate when asked if he ever felt like he needed another "guy" around the house. "Of course not," he said with conviction.

Jennifer did admit it was tough trying to raise Chris—and to understand a male point of view—as he got older. It's not that he is a boy, but his personality and approach to things are so different than the girls' and not in a bad way," Jennifer said. "The older he gets, the more apparent the differences in how he approaches things and how he does things are, and sometimes we are good at adjusting our way of thinking to realize that."

Maggie, now 21, said she feels close to Chris mainly because she's nearest to him in age. Like her older sisters, Maggie graduated from St. V-M (2003). She is in her third year in the nursing program at Kent State University and is a nurse's assistant at Akron General Medical Center.

"Chris and I were always close, and we'll always be referred to as 'the kids' because we were always the kids when my parents were alive," said Maggie, who made it to Chris' Senior Night later in the evening.

"I think as I get older, I feel more responsibility toward him, more of a mother, like Jen and Becky do. Before, he was just my little brother."

Chris has been involved in sports constantly since a very young age. He has played everything—soccer, baseball, football, basketball—you name it, and we have always gone to the games," Jennifer said. "And even when the girls were younger, it was just the family thing to do. You always go to the game, but I have to say with Chris in high school football, the older he got, the more excited I got watching him because we have watched how hard he has worked over the years."

Chris wasn't a starter on this season's 4-6 Irish team. He got limited playing time but was determined to finish his senior year on the team. He said his interaction with his neighborhood friends somewhat helped him bond with male figures because he was, and still is, the only male living in a household with three women.

"Our neighborhood, for one, was really close," Chris said about growing up in the North Hill section of Akron. "There were a lot of kids on our street, so I had a lot of friends and we played football and all kinds of sports all the time."

Jennifer and her siblings said that after their parents' deaths, people occasionally formed misconceptions about her family. "I'm sure some people thought this was going to be a party house, and that wasn't the case at all," Jennifer said. "Don't get me wrong, even when the kids were younger, we each filled a different role as far as what it takes to run a family. Becky is my cleaner/organizer. I mean at 16, Becky would change everyone's winter clothes to summer clothes."

(Just as Jennifer was describing how responsible Becky always has been, Becky was cleaning everyone's dishes from the kitchen table after dinner.)

"When I would come home from a date and mom and dad were still sleeping, there would be a note from Becky that said, 'Jen, please make sure all the windows and doors are locked.'"

Added Maggie: "I remember Becky crying the entire night Jen turned 21 because she thought Jen was going to drink."

"See, Maggie is my comic relief," Jennifer added.

Then Chris said, jokingly, "And I'm her sunshine."

Jennifer responded, "Yeah, Chris is my gentle soul."

What makes this atypical family so special is how it came together in the face of tragedy to become so strong, loving and caring for one another. "Maybe when you stop and look at what we've been through and where we are, you might say it was amazing, but we have never thought about it any other way than just we were going to take care of one another," Becky said.

Jennifer commented: "As the kids get older and they start achieving their own accomplishments as individuals and adults, like graduating from high school, college, then getting jobs, I am like, 'Wow, I guess we did do a good job.' Because everyone's life is on a steady course forward.

"I guess as they get older, I look at the three of them and say not only did they survive losing mom and dad, but they survived me and they have gone on to achieve great things and be good people."

Jennifer recalled the waves of emotion as she, Chris and Becky walked across the field and heard his name announced over the public address system during the Senior Night festivities. "It was a very bittersweet night for all of us," Jennifer said. "As we walked out on the field and heard 'Christopher House, son of the late Bill and Betsy' we all paused for a moment."

Chris played on the kickoff and punt teams that night and made the most of the last home game of his high school football career. "As I watched Chris, whether running a play or standing on the sideline, I realized that this was the last time I would be watching him play at St. V," Jennifer said. "As the lump in my throat formed, I couldn't help but think of how much he had grown, physically and emotionally, compared to the first time I watched him play at St. V. I was proud of him and for him. As with all of the kids, I knew Mom and Dad would be proud."

AUTHOR'S INSPIRATION

Just through my experience covering St. Vincent-St. Mary athletics over the years, several people close to the school and the program always told me that I needed to do a story on Chris House, a football player who lost both of his parents when he was young. They told me that the older sister, Jennifer, wanted to keep the family together so she filed papers to adopt her younger siblings (they had the same parents) so that the family could stay together.

That act of unselfish, unconditional love for her siblings was amazing to me. Jennifer was in her early 20s and while most of her friends were enjoying college life, Jennifer was taking on a monumental responsibility of caring for her family, fulfilling the wishes of her late parents. She has made her parents proud.

Tallmadge Family Bands Together: Blue Devils Athlete Envisions One Day Marching for OSU

Fascinating, dynamic, upbeat.

Words that could describe Jonathan Lampley, a National Merit Scholarship finalist who is class vice president at Tallmadge High School. He has a 4.2 grade-point average, plays on the basketball team, and participates in the marching (tuba) and concert (trumpet) bands and the drama club.

Committed, determined, focused.

Next year, Lampley will attend Ohio State and plans to be a doctor. Almost as important as Lampley's goal of graduating with a medical degree is his goal to become a member of Ohio State's marching band "The Best Damn Band in the Land."

"When I was 7 years old, I was with my parents at an Ohio State game and that was the first time I started loving Ohio State," he said. "I loved the football team and the band. But my goal is to 'dot the i' when I'm at Ohio State." That means being a senior sousaphone player and having the privilege of high-stepping his way out from the Script Ohio to become the individual who makes a crowd of 100,000-plus at Ohio Stadium go crazy. Lampley eagerly awaited this school year, expecting to enjoy the time of his life as a senior in high school.

"I was very excited about my senior year because everyone talks about how fast it goes," he said. "So I want to make the best of every day and enjoy being around my friends, my classmates and my teammates. I'll never have this time back again, so I want to make the very best of it."

Supportive, considerate, caring.

Then, early this school year, came news regarding his mother, Rebekah: a diagnosis of breast cancer. "We had open house at the school and I had a doctor's appointment that day," Rebekah Lampley said. "I went back to school and informed some people that I had breast cancer, and it has been a journey from the first day of September until now.

"I have chemotherapy on Fridays, then I go to Jonathan's games," she said. "Jonathan would always come over to me after games and would be so supportive and considerate and would ask how I was doing. This journey has not been easy for any of us, but Jonathan has been awesome."

Rebekah said her illness has helped the family understand the importance of life. "Since I've been sick, I haven't been on them to pick up their socks because it hasn't mattered for the last four months," she said, jokingly, speaking as a mother who likes to keep her house clean when others in her house, namely her husband and son, don't. Everybody is taking a break because we now realize that the little stuff in life really doesn't matter," she said. "All the little stuff we worry about every day in our lives really doesn't matter."

Rebekah Lampley said she has her "good days and bad days" with chemotherapy treatment. She said she makes it through with the support of her family and friends, especially those at First Apostolic Faith Church. Her son looks at her as his hero.

"I think it's amazing how positive she stays throughout her whole ordeal," Jonathan said. "She has her treatments on Fridays but she's still at every one of my games, and that means a lot." Jonathan Lampley's father, also named Jonathan, is awaiting a kidney transplant and undergoes dialysis three days a week. "I have chronic kidney failure and I'm in the process of waiting for a kidney transplant," he said. "It has been challenging, sometimes, to go to games because I go to dialysis Monday, Wednesday and Friday and I don't have much strength sometimes after dialysis, and most of Jonathan's games are on Fridays.

"But when I see the spirit Jonathan has and the way he works with his mom and I, with the health problems we have, it's just so amazing. He doesn't let our problems affect him. It's uplifting for my wife and I, because all of the hard work that we've done with him and all of the hard work he's done has come to fruition. He's a very good kid, and even if he wasn't my son, to see how much of a leader he is is something I admire. When you see any young kid with his head in the right direction, it's inspiring."

The younger Lampley added: "My mom and dad have supported me in everything I've ever done . . . What's really helped me be successful is knowing that no matter what I do, I'll always have their support." On the basketball court, Lampley is a hard worker and leader for coach Jon Karnuth. The Blue Devils (14-6) will face Suburban League rival Revere in the Division II sectional tournament Saturday afternoon at Stow.

During the regular season, Lampley averaged 13.5 points and 6.5 rebounds per game. He finished the regular season with 50 points and 29 rebounds in the final three games.

"Jonathan brings this competitive spirit and I haven't had anyone like that other than Alan Bock," Karnuth said, referring to an outstanding 2002 Tallmadge graduate. "Jonathan is going to give you 100 percent at all times. "But the great thing about him is he's well-respected. He's probably the most well-rounded kid I've ever been around. He's the lead in the school play, he plays different instruments, he's outstanding in the classroom, and the most amazing thing is how humble he is. He's so reserved about his abilities." Rebekah Lampley said that might be her son's one fault.

"Jonathan entered this poetry contest in school one time where he recited poetry," she said. "He ended up winning second prize and he never even told me. He didn't even invite me. "I asked him, 'Jonathan, why didn't you invite me?' He said he didn't think it was a big deal. And that's Jonathan. He doesn't think any of his accomplishments are a big deal, but we do. To us, he's a gift from God. I call him 'the Midas-touch boy' because everything he touches turns to gold."

Tallmadge Principal Rebecca DeCapua summed it up simply: "Jonathan is just a phenomenal young man."

AUTHOR'S INSPIRATION

Jonathan was one of the most mild-mannered, intelligent, caring and all-around talented people I've ever met. He was an amazing student in the classroom and a hard worker on the basketball court. But he never let his parent's health issues get him—or them—down. He was their strength through difficult times. What I admired most about Jonathan was that he always had a positive and up-beat attitude no matter what was going on in his life, which is why so many of his classmates and friends enjoyed being in his company. He's a member of the Ohio State Marching Band, "The Best Damn Band in the Land."

Diversity, Golf Meet: Every Young Golfer Given Chance to Play at Akron's First Tee

They were young boys and girls. They were white, black and Asian. They were from the city, the suburbs and the country. Some came from families who were well-off financially, and others weren't. But none of that mattered. It usually never matters when you're talking about kids . . . and golf.

A sport that in the past was looked upon as elitist has shed that image, thanks to programs like Akron's First Tee at Mud Run Golf Course. Program director David Alexander said the sport can teach young people about life. First Tee is designed to "positively impact young people through programs that promote positive character development and life-enhancing values through the game of golf."

Alexander said he has 240 participants, from ages 8 to 18, in the program, which runs through the fall, and they are divided into different skill levels. They have instructions twice a week and are able to play a full round of golf four times a week for free. What's most important about the program are the nine core values taught: honesty, integrity, sportsmanship, respect, confidence, responsibility, perseverance, courtesy and judgment.

K. Strobelt-McCann from Copley Township, a mother of eight who were all brought together through adoption, has four children in the program: sisters Emma, who is Asian and 11 years old, and Tesha, who is black and 9, are two. "It would be wonderful if the girls were good enough to get scholarships," said Strobelt-McCann, who is a 43-year-old white woman. "Then they could trace their history back to David Alexander and First Tee and come back and give back to the program. David welcomed us with open arms, and he's doing great and wonderful things with the kids."

The interesting thing about Strobelt-McCann is that she's never played the sport in her life."'I don't know anything about it," said Strobelt-McCann, whose extended van has a licence plate that reads, "Mom To 8."

"I always thought it was a sport that wealthy people could do and I wasn't wealthy so I could never do it," she said. "I wanted my kids to have all the opportunities in the world, no matter what, and I don't want them not to pursue those opportunities because they are girls, or because of their race, or because they may not be rich."

Strobelt-McCann said she learned about First Tee from friends. She went to the Web site and was pleasantly surprised with what the program offered. "It's not only about golf," she said. "The program teaches the kids how to greet people and how to respect people and treat them the right way, the core values of life." Kelsey Weber lives in Akron and will be a sophomore golfer at Medina High next season. Weber is exactly the type of young person First Tee represents. She started in the program four years ago and improved each year. Last year, she was named the program's Most Valuable Female Golfer.

When Kelsey's group finished their instruction session for the day, she stayed to help out the younger group. "I just feel that it's the right thing to do," Weber said. "I usually help out the younger girls because when I was their age, there really weren't any girls here to kind of help me out. So I think that's important." One of the things that Alexander does each session is have his participants introduce themselves to those who might be new to the program. For Cyler Caldwell, a 13-year-old from Wadsworth, that lesson carries into his life off the course.

"Whenever we have a new kid come to our school, I always go up to them and say 'hi' and ask them their name," Cyler said. "I just want to make them feel welcome. I learned that here (at First Tee.)" Inside First Tee's meeting room, Alexander was busy doing his normal routine, handing out clubs to kids who didn't have any, signing up new golfers and making sure everyone's needs were met. Over Alexander's shoulder high on the wall was a huge banner provided by the USGA with recent U.S. Open champion Tiger Woods on the left end and LPGA star Michelle Wie on the right. Alexander said the banner is the perfect symbol for what the program, and the sport, have become.

"We have kids from every race, class, economic background and that's what's so great about the program," he said. "We have kids whose parents are members of country clubs and those who aren't and it doesn't matter to them, or us, because we're bringing them all together to learn to play a great sport." After one group of young golfers ended their day, they walked into the clubhouse anxiously awaiting the opportunity to buy the popular special a $1 hot dog. In fact, one adult volunteer joked about the deal.

"Austin (Griffith) lived off those hot dogs all summer long last year," the volunteer said about Griffith, a seventh-grader from Barberton. "You know how some young kids are considered gym rats during basketball season? Well, Austin is like most of these kids. He's a course rat." Meanwhile, inside, 9-year-old Jordan Esterle, of Manchester, who is white, was sitting at a table in the clubhouse enjoying a hot dog with a another young girl, who was black. The two girls never met each other until Tuesday. But they acted as if they had been friends for years. They even exchanged phone numbers and made plans to visit each other's houses.

Neither saw color. Only friendship and fun.

"I like coming here because I meet new people," Jordan said. "I can't wait to come back next week and meet my new friend again."

AUTHOR'S INSPIRATION

The game of golf used to represent affluence and an elitist attitude by those who were fortunate enough to play the game. Thanks to so many—from Charlie Sifford to Tiger Woods—golf isn't a game just for whites.

Doing stories on The First Tee of Akron Program always makes me feel good because when I go out to golf courses, it's great to see boys and girls of all ages and races coming together to enjoy a sport that used to have racial overtones. They are still there, but not as strong.

Boy Tosses Aside Early Limitations: Akron Teen Defies Odds to Become Outstanding Pitcher, First Baseman

When you're sitting on the bench next to 13-year-old Greg Rybka, it is possible to see in his eyes, as he talks about baseball, just how much he loves the game.

As he chews on his mouthpiece and gazes through the fence out to the field, you can sense the determination and dedication he puts into the game.

Greg plays for the Indians, the F League (13-to-14 age group), of the West Akron Baseball League, known as WABL. He's an outstanding first baseman and one of the team's top pitchers.

He also was born without the lower part of his legs and with only one fully functioning arm. When Greg was 2, his parents, Kelly and Bob, had him fitted with prosthetic legs and he has been running wild ever since. "It was good we decided early [on the prosthetics], because otherwise I would have grown up and would have been self-conscious about it," Greg said. "Since I was at an age where I can't remember much when I got them, I think that helped, because this is all I've ever known, so I just go out and try to do my best."

The Rybkas' other six children, including 4-year-old John Paul and 8-year-old Peter, who love to go to the ballpark more for the enjoyment of burying themselves in mounds of dirt, are proud of Greg's accomplishments on the baseball field.

Kelly Rybka said Greg is a role model to everyone in his family. "I think God gave him a natural ability to go out and just do things for himself," Kelly said. "We didn't teach him to tie his shoes. He figured it out himself. All the things that most of us never think about, like pulling up your pants, he had to learn to do that on his own when he was young. He would never let anything stop him."

So, as I watched Greg drill a ball up the middle for an RBI single (he was 2-for-3 and his team won 16-7 that night), and as I watched him field a ground ball, and as I watched him run the bases and field balls at first, all I could think about was how *normal* he was. He was playing baseball, the Great American Pastime, and enjoying every inning, like a lot of kids across the country do, because that's all Greg wants to be, like most *normal* kids across the country.

"Playing sports boosted my self-confidence," said Greg, who also played basketball at St. Mary Grade School. He'll attend St. Vincent-St. Mary this fall and said he'll stop playing basketball so he can continue his dream of playing high school baseball. "I just like being out here and helping my team win. That's what I love the most," he said.

I'm sure every opposing coach would have made Greg one of his top draft picks because the young man can play the game. More important, he has a positive attitude toward life that is contagious.

And today will be a special day for Greg. The West Akron Baseball League is having its annual recognition day this afternoon at Canal Park before the Aeros' game against the Portland Sea Dogs. WABL players and their parents, family and friends will be special guests at the stadium.

And guess whose 14th birthday is today?

And guess who's throwing out the first pitch?

You guessed right—Greg Rybka, and on this day, there's no one more deserving.

AUTHOR'S INSPIRATION

When a friend of mine, Mike Dies, told me that he had a great inspirational story, I couldn't wait to hear it. So when I met Greg, I was absolutely impressed with this young man. He was born without the lower parts of his leg and with one functional arm, but he has never let that stop him from doing all the things his peers do. His outlook on life is something we should all share.

Meanwhile, one email I received about the story came from a man in Texas. It proves that stories like Greg's have a ripple effect that can travel and inspire others thousands of miles away.

Dear Mr. Morgan,

I am a High School Baseball Coach in Sour Lake, Texas. I have been coaching, umpiring, and playing Baseball for over 25 years. I am the pitching coach at an area high school and have been a Head Baseball coach in the past. I was very inspired by your story on Greg Rybka. My interest comes from the fact that I too was born with a congenital birth defect. The umbilical cord wrapped around my right arm and didn't allow it to form properly. I would like to get in contact with the Rybka's. Would you please pass on my email address to them and ask them to contact me. I grew up thinking I was the only person with this kind of problem and would like to initiate a dialog with young Greg to, hopefully, inspire him to continue his dream of playing high school baseball.

Sincerely,

Todd Moses
Pitching Coach
Beaumont West Brook High School

CHAPTER 2

DEDICATION

Giving Up Not Option to Dedicated Revere Boys

For one day, the Revere boys basketball team walked the halls of their school with pride. They were winners. Naturally, the 14 members of the varsity team are all winners, but now, at least, it was reflected in their record.

On Tuesday, the Minutemen finally managed to notch that elusive first win, after starting the season with 12 consecutive losses. It was a 61-59 overtime victory against Suburban League foe Wadsworth. I'm sure before the season started, players like 6-foot-3 senior forward Wayne Whitmore and 6-2 senior forward Scott Lauck never thought it would take until late January to get win No. 1.

"Losing 12 straight games was frustrating and it was tough going through that," Whitmore said. "It would have been easy for me to quit and go get a job or something. But none of us ever quit. We kept fighting and working hard in practice because we lost a lot of games that were close." Lauck said: "I just didn't let it get to me because we always played hard. We finally just put it all together."

The sad truth is that winning is everything. In an idealistic world, we wouldn't put so much emphasis on winning. Realists, however, live by the adage that someone has to win and someone has to lose, and winning means being a success. If you win, you're a success; if you lose, you're not.

I don't think that way. The ability to handle adversity, whether it's a loss, or not being able to attain a particular goal, is a life lesson that ultimately will help you win or attain that particular goal in the future. Someone I look up to gave me a book a few years ago that was full of inspirational sayings from famous, not-so-famous and even some anonymous people. That book, which you can't buy in any bookstore, is called the *Winner's Manual*.

As I looked through the book recently among the hundreds of inspirational sayings, one grabbed my attention. It was from Elie Wiesel, a Romanian-born writer and Holocaust survivor who won the Nobel Peace Prize in 1986. When I read in the paper that Revere had won its first game, I realized that Wiesel's quote embodies the Minutemen's hard work, determination and perseverance this year.

> *Nobody is stronger . . . than someone who came back. There is nothing you can do to such a person because whatever you could do is less than what has already been done to him.*

Without hearing the quote, Whitmore said almost the same thing. "I can look at what I've been through and know that nothing can hold me back now," he said. "Because I've been through so much, I won't be afraid to lose anymore, as long as I always work hard."

Lauck added: "This whole season taught me to never give up or quit and to always keep going." Imagine how these players felt practicing every day only to come up short game after game. "It was a great feeling to walk into school today," Whitmore said Wednesday. "Everybody was congratulating us."

No matter what happens the rest of the season, it can't get any worse. It can only get better. So for those of you who can relate to Revere's experiences, remember Wiesel's quote, along with some of the following, and you're sure to be winners in the game of life.

> *You have to accept whatever comes and the only important thing is that you meet it with courage and with the best that you have to give.*
> *—Eleanor Roosevelt*

> *A certain amount of opposition is a great help to man. Kites rise against, not with, the wind.*
> *—American writer John Neal*

> *Our greatest glory is not in never failing, but rising every time we fall.*
> *—Confucius*

> *The ultimate measure of a man is not where he stands in moments of comfort and convenience, but where he stands at times of challenge and controversy.*
> *—Martin Luther King Jr*

> *Shoulda, coulda and woulda won't get it done. In attacking adversity, only a positive attitude, alertness and regrouping to basics can launch a comeback.*
> *—Miami Heat coach Pat Riley*

AUTHOR'S INSPIRATION

I was looking at boxscores one morning while drinking coffee and I noticed that Revere's boys basketball team had won its first game of the season. My first thought was that those young men had to feel a great sense of relief. Think about it. In today's sports culture, with the emphasis always on winning, to finally get that first of the year had to be a special feeling.

I picked up the telephone, called the school and told the secretary that I wanted to write a positive column about that ONE win. Sure it was one win. But it meant more than that. After 12 straight losses, players could have pointed fingers, laid blame or even just quit. They didn't.

Ellet QB Leffler Gets Call: Freshman Might Be Small on Size, but Big Heart Makes Up for It

The following phone conversation took place last night at the home of Ellet freshman Mark Leffler, the Orangemen's starting varsity quarterback:

Reporter: "This is the Beacon Journal, *is Mark there?"*

Annie Leffler (Mark's sister): "Are you serious? OK, hold on . . . MAAAAARKKK! It's the Beacon Journal. *They want to talk to you."*

Mark: "Yeah, right!"

Annie: "I'm serious. Pick it up!"

Reporter: "Hello, Mark, I'm with the Beacon Journal.*"*

Mark: "Yeah, right. Who is this, really?"

Reporter: It's the Beacon Journal, *Mark.*

You think this hasn't been an unbelievable season for Mark Leffler? And if football is about courage, determination and heart, then Leffler is the gridiron poster boy. Last year, Leffler was in the same building with kindergartners, as an eighth-grader at St. Matthew School. But this year, he's the starting varsity quarterback for Ellet.

Leffler, all 5-foot-7, 132-pounds of him, will lead the Orangemen offense against Nordonia this week. Leffler was thrust into the starting role last week against Lake after senior Justin Palmer injured his shoulder in a scrimmage a few weeks ago. Palmer could return in the next few weeks, but for now, Leffler is the man. "Mark is a very talented player and he showed a great deal of poise and courage for a kid starting in is first varsity game as a freshman," Ellet coach Joe Yost said of Leffler's performance in a 20-0 loss to an outstanding Lake team. "I think they (Lake) had to respect the fact that Mark looked them right in the eye and didn't back down."

There's no fear in Leffler's heart.

OK, maybe there was a little fear, but it's gone now.

"Before the game, while I was in the fieldhouse at Lake, I was so nervous," he said. "I was like that until we got on the field and after that, I was fine." There is, however, some fear in Leffler's mom's heart. "I'm happy for him because he's a hard worker but on the other hand, I'm a little scared because he's so young and so small," Denise Leffler said. "I did give him some advice. I told him to get rid of the ball."

Mark Leffler's dad, Tom, said: "We were surprised he was the starting JV quarterback this season. But when Justin got hurt and they made Mark the starter, it was incredible. When he runs out there with all the other guys, he looks like a stick. But Joe (Yost) wouldn't have Mark out there if he didn't think he could do the job." To say things have happened really fast for Leffler and his family is an understatement. His sister, Annie, is a senior at Ellet and the class president. And she had no idea that her kid brother would arrive at high school and have one of the most important jobs on the football team.

But Leffler is taking it all in stride. "I thought her friends would pick on me and stuff like that because I'm a freshman, but they've all been really nice to me," he said. "I still look up to Annie."

Annie Leffler returns the praise. "We're all very proud of Mark but we're all in shock, too," she said. "He came home from practices last week and said he was doing really well and that he might be starting, but we never imagined it would be this soon."

But then, it has been an unbelievable season for Leffler and his family.

AUTHOR'S INSPIRATION

When coach Yost told me that he was going to be starting a freshman at quarterback to start the season, I instantly thought "FEATURE STORY." Mainly because the last thing a high school coach wants to do is give the varsity starting quarterback job to a freshman. Someone who probably just threw out the last pair of Underoos he had stashed away in the bottom of his underwear drawer.

Not that Leffler was an Underoos man instead of Hanes, it's just that freshmen in general are just trying to fit in the first year. But there was Leffler, having to do more than just fit in. I felt the courage he showed in stepping in was admirable.

Dream Becomes a Tall Order: Hudson Girl Outgrows Skating, Finds Success on Basketball Court

We all dream. And the dream that floated in the head of Hudson senior basketball player Maggie Kopnisky as a little girl was magical: to one day become an Olympic figure skater. The dream was not at all far-fetched. Kopnisky, a starting forward for the Hudson team that will take on Kenmore tonight, was an accomplished figure skater until a few years ago, when she reluctantly gave up the sport. Kopnisky loves the sports she's into now, basketball and track, but ice skating, well . . .

She began skating at age 5, when her mother, Kathy, took her to the rink at Kent State for recreational skating. Kopnisky instantly fell in love with the sport. "I had big goals and big dreams, and one of my dreams was to skate in the Olympics," she said. "I really loved skating, and when I was about 7, I started taking private lessons."

Those private lessons meant early morning drives to Gilmour Academy in Gates Mills for ice time. And when Kathy Kopnisky says early, she means early. "We would get up at 4:30 in the morning, and I would drive Maggie to Gilmour Academy during the winter, and there was always a lot of snow up there," Kathy Kopnisky said. "Once we got there, the only people there were Maggie and I, and the guy who opened the rink. Maggie and I wouldn't talk during the ride there, and once we got there and she went inside, the place was completely silent. Then she would turn on *NSYNC's *Bye, Bye, Bye* and skate. And the music would rock the rafters. That will always be a nice mom memory for me."

Said Maggie Kopnisky: "My mom was awesome during that whole time. She was always there for me and drove me to practice every day." Over the course of her years as a skater, she won awards and medals and met or skated with some of the biggest names in the sport: world champions Kimmie Meissner, Tara Lipinski and Rosalynn Sumners, who choreographed some of Kopnisky's routines during her competitions.

"When I skated in Strongsville, Rosalynn worked with a lot of us because I think her fiance was from this area so she was here a lot," Kopnisky said. "I also met a lot of people in the sport when I would go to Scott Hamilton's cancer event every year."

A trip to the U.S. Olympic Training center in Colorado Springs, Colo., with other aspiring Olympic hopefuls and their parents changed things for Kopnisky's parents. "We talked to an Olympic trainer there as a group and he talked about how when a female skater hits 90 pounds and does triple jumps, it's hard on the female skeleton," Kathy Kopnisky said. "That's when my husband (Jack) and I thought, 'What is our role as parents? Do we want our daughter to have to worry about injuries like that?' "

Maggie Kopnisky had been a petite skater, but she was growing quickly and was close to 90 pounds at the time they heard the trainer's warning. "I used to be little, and most skaters are almost like gymnasts-size because of the routines and the jumps that you do," said Kopnisky, who is now 5-foot-10. "It has to do with your center of gravity when you're small. Then I had a growth spurt about my eighth-grade year. Once I got tall, I realized I couldn't skate anymore, so I wanted to play basketball and run track."

Kopnisky said her regimented skating program during the years has made her a better basketball player. "We did a lot of off-ice training . . . things like ballet, and that really helped me with my flexibility and agility," she said. "One four-minute program is like playing an entire basketball game." Kopnisky is a starter for coach Dennis Lawler and has developed into a quality player.

"We try to use Maggie's athleticism and she usually draws the opponent's best players because she's our quickest defender," Lawler said. "She's so quick and so long, she makes it hard for opponents to get their shot off." And Lawler said Kopnisky is a special young lady off the court, as well.

"She's a great kid who does well in the classroom," he said. "She's well-liked on the team but also in school, and she's just a really fun person to be around."

Kathy Kopnisky said she knows her daughter misses skating, but she also knows she has become a more dynamic person because of her experience on the ice. "In her college essay, Maggie wrote about how she missed skating and how skating was her identity," Kathy Kopnisky said. "She said when she decided to stop skating, she was a little afraid. But now she plays basketball and runs track, and she could not have done any of that if she continued on with her skating. She's really a hard worker, and we're proud of her."

AUTHOR'S INSPIRATION

This amazing story came out of nowhere. I was covering Maggie's basketball team during a state tournament game and it impressed me that she moved so well on the court for her size (5-10). She was so fluid running up and down the court and you don't see that very often for a post player.

After the game, I went to the coach, Tony Whitmer, and told him I was impressed with the way Maggie runs the court. Tony said, "I have to tell you a secret. She used to be an amazing figure skater and was in the Olympic Development program."

I was blown away. But then I realized that it made sense. That's why she looked so good on the basketball court. Her figure skating training helped with her transition from the ice to the court. It was a great story that I may have otherwise not known about if I hadn't asked Tony about Maggie. And so often, some of the best stories come from just a nugget of information that turns out to be a jewel.

Swimmer Dives Into Life After Team

They awaken at 5 in the morning, sometimes even earlier, in the dead of winter, knowing it's a commitment they made to themselves, to their teammates and to the sport of swimming.

Those morning practices are grueling. When most people are still slapping the snooze button for the umpteenth time, these high school swimmers and divers already have put in dozens and dozens and dozens of laps or countless twists and flips from the springboard.

Then it's off to class for the day, only to return to the pool after school for another practice session. Swimmers in Northeast Ohio are dedicated to their sport beyond comprehension. They will do whatever it takes to not only be the best they can be, but also to give the best effort they can give. That's what high school swimming is all about.

Recently, the Firestone diving coach sent me a copy of a letter from 1992 Firestone High graduate Dan Waterman, who was a member of the Falcons swim team. Waterman, who lives in Colorado, sent this letter to current Firestone coach Cindy Virdo.

After reading his letter, and understanding how much his experience as a swimmer at Firestone changed his life, my only thought was that his message needed to be shared. Make sure there are no distractions or interruptions when you read this, then share it with someone else. You'll be glad you did.

Hello Cindy. My name is Dan Waterman, a 1992 *graduate from Firestone High. I just wanted to touch base with you since the Firestone swim team changed my life for the better. After high school, I never let go of the need for competition, the fight, endurance and pushing myself as hard as I could. For any swimmers struggling with practices right now, I share with you my personal victory.*

You won't see my name on any record board or in the showcase outside the pool. However, what you don't see is the heart of a champion inside me that was slowly constructed through years of punishment.

I started as a sophomore, out of shape, and teased for my inability to keep up with the "fast lanes." Not until my final event my senior year, after my father told me to leave nothing behind after my 100*-yard freestyle, did I fully understand what a champion commits to him or herself.*

I climbed on my block at districts with one thing going through my mind, leaving nothing behind. I couldn't hear the crowd, I didn't feel my nerves and the only thing I could think of was hitting that placid water with everything I had.

To this day, I watch the footage my Dad took. I watch it in slow motion to watch as every swimmer hits the water and I am still in flight, soaring as a Falcon, I guess you can say.

All I can remember is on the final 25 *yards, I couldn't feel my arms and was only hoping that as my instincts kicked in, my arms would propel me forward. Upon touching the wall, I gasped for air high into the sky and looked for the time on the wall above the diving boards.*

It was 53.00.

I shot my right fist into the air knowing full well I was a champion. My time held up as the top time for 10 *more heats. This may not seem like much to some of the amazing swimmers at Firestone, but it was incredible to me.*

You see, the best I'd ever done was 58.00, and that was on a good day. I stepped out of that pool and into the parade of high-fives from teammates such as Todd and Tim Tober, Neill Barger, George Hitler, Mike Teter, Dan Able, Gene Fitch, Tim Lewarchick, Kristof Batizy, Emily Aberth, Neal Small, Nick Albrect, A.J. Sands, Jamie Hunt and most importantly, my little brother, Mike, who was an impressionable freshman.

Through the three years I spent on the Firestone swim team . . . the only regret that I have is that I didn't start earlier in life.

AUTHOR'S INSPIRATION

A friend of mine is a diving coach at a local high school. One day she contacted me about a letter the head swim coach received from a former diver. This young man had moved away to Colorado after graduating from high school and was doing well for himself in the business world. But he felt compelled to write a letter to his former swim coach and share the fact that his experience on the swim team had a big impact on his life. I felt his story is what dedication and determination is all about as a high school athlete, whether you're a starter or on third string. The lessons you learn as a high school student-athlete will remain with you the rest of your life and will carry into all endeavors you face, personally and professionally.

I think Dan's letter said it all.

Woodridge Junior Scoring Off Court: Murphy Gets Early Start in Business World With T-Shirt Sales, Dances

"Hello . . . you have reached Mylan Murphy . . . founder and president of Novel Clothing Co. . . . Please leave him a message and he will get back with you as soon as convenient . . . Thank you, and have a great day."

That's not the voice-mail of a successful corporate tycoon. It's the computer-generated voice-mail of Mylan Murphy, entrepreneur and 16-year-old junior at Woodridge High. Murphy also is an outstanding basketball player, a 6-foot-6 center for the Bulldogs (6-5 overall, 5-2 in the Portage Trail Conference County Division).

Murphy is averaging 17.5 points and 12.5 rebounds. His averages were 14 points and seven rebounds last season. Away from basketball, Murphy's business interest started with a love of drawing. He started Novel Clothing Co. at the end of his eighth-grade year. His clothes consists of T-shirts with three different logos he designed.

The designs have slogans like "To Be Unusual," "Unlocking the Future," and "Escaping the Past." They sell for $10 each. Murphy said after doing some research "on how I could get my designs printed on T-shirts," he found a print shop and started selling products.

Murphy's revenue from sales isn't going to make him a millionaire—at least not right now. This past summer, Murphy had 150 shirts printed, his biggest order at one time, and sold them at events such as the King of the Court basketball tournament attended by LeBron James at Perkins Park.

He also sent shirts to Dayton with his business partner and older brother, Mike, who was a football player at the University of Dayton. Mike said his customers liked the designs. "There were a few fashion shows at Dayton, Wright State, Wilberforce (University) and Central State where me and some buddies would sell the articles," Mike said. "We even won second place at a show at Wright State. Since Mylan is young, I try to do some of things he can't. He has a vision and I try make it happen."

Mylan said he's sold about 700 T-shirts since his startup. For him, it's about expressing his creativity. "I always saw famous people with their own clothing lines and I decided I wanted to do the same thing," he said. "I always buy (Michael) Jordan's stuff that comes out and now LeBron's, so I looked into doing my own thing. I wanted to be different and have things other people didn't."

Mylan's mother, Terri Murphy, says he was born with a desire to show his creativity and individuality. "When I was pregnant with him, I dreamed I was going to have a son and I dreamed that when he was born, he came out in a green suit," she said. "And in this green suit, Mylan said, 'Everybody will have to accept me how I am.' He's a very confident, independent kid who gets along with everyone."

Woodridge coach Dave Krusinski says, "He's just a gentleman at the age of 16 and he handles himself like an adult. He's reaching out already. The kid's got it together and from a basketball standpoint, he's learning to be a leader. He works hard every day and never misses a day of practice. As a coach, it's a dream to have a kid like that."

Not only is Mylan in the clothing business, he's in the entertainment business, as well. He also has started Novel Entertainment. "I'll rent out a hall for a high school dance, then I'll have 'hot cards' printed up, which are postcards that have the time, place and price of admission and I send those out," he said.

So far, Mylan, with the help of his brother, has held two parties with no incidents.

"Doing the parties is something new that we tried out," Mike said. "We needed to do something to raise money to make the clothing so we had a party around Thanksgiving and another around Christmas."

Meanwhile, on the basketball court, Mylan is working hard to become a Division I college prospect. His goal is to play in college ball while studying business.

"When I finish college, I want to expand my business beyond clothing," Mylan said.

AUTHOR'S INSPIRATION

Mylan was another one of those kids I knew in the neighborhood who was always respectful, polite and did well in school. He was also very talented as an athlete so I knew he had lots of potential. I also knew he would eventually do something positive with his life, I just didn't know what it would be.

While in high school, Mylan called me one day and left a message for me to call him. I thought he was going to ask me to cover one of his games or something like that, because as much of a great kid Mylan was, he was always asking for "publicity." Like, "Mr. Morgan, when are you going to come to our game and give us some pub?"

That was Mylan, very outgoing, confident and sure of himself. And in absolutely no way was he cocky. I eventually returned Mylan's call and I got a voicemail that sounded like a secretary of a Fortune 500 company. That's when I first learned about Mylan's amazing entrepreneurial skills and vision. I though it was imperative to write a story about Mylan being such an ambitious teenager trying to make a name for himself in the business world.

On Stage or in Stadium, Athleticism Counts: Teen Calls Dance a Tough Sport

Sweat poured off the face of Dominic Moore as the music played. The song was *Neutron Dance* by the Pointer Sisters, from the *Beverly Hills Cop* soundtrack. Moore, a Firestone High School sophomore, and about 25 members of the Studio West Performing Arts Center in Akron were practicing a tap routine for a national competition in Cincinnati to be held later this month.

The two-hour practice was part of Moore's schedule just one day before he had to go to Columbus to run in the 110- and 300-meter hurdles races at the Division I state track meet at Ohio State University.

If that sounds like a packed schedule, take note that Moore also found time to play defender for Greater Akron Premier U-18 soccer in a State Cup semifinal match on the Monday before the state track meet.

The Akron club plays teams from northern Ohio in soccer's "off" season.

"During track season, every week changes," Moore said. "I'm supposed to be at soccer practice from 4 to 6 (P.M.) Monday through Wednesday and dance from 4:30 to 8 (P.M.) and I still have to fit track in there. I guess I just wiggle my way through everything to make sure I give everything equal time."

The busy week leading up to state track in Columbus didn't seem to affect Moore at all. He capped off the year by placing fourth in the 300 hurdles and seventh in the 110 hurdles. The weeks leading up to state were a track success, too. During a three-week stretch in May, Moore was second in the 110 and first in the 300 at the City Series meet, second in both at the district meet and second (300) and third (110) at the regional meet.

"Man, going to state wasn't even in my mind at the beginning of the season," Moore said. "I was just worried about running against people in the City (Series). To be honest, I never thought I'd get through districts.

"Now that I look back on everything, it was a great season. As the season went on, I got a lot better and my times started dropping." When Moore first thought about the hurdles, he wasn't sure he was doing the right thing. He had been a sprinter.

But he put together the mentality and mechanics to learn the new event.

"All you can say about Dominic is that he's a terrific kid," Firestone coach Matt Beaven said. "He cut a second off his time from last year in the 110 (hurdles). His best time last year was a 15.7 and his best time this year was 14.36."

Moore's seventh-place time in the 110 at state was 14.85. Moore said he decided to go high-tech to help him become a better hurdler. "One of the things that helped me a lot was going online and watching people run hurdles and looking at their form," he said.

Form is obviously important to Moore in dancing, too. That career started when he was 2½ years old. "He's a natural," said Mark Smith, owner of Studio West with his wife Erin, who also teaches dance at Kent State University. Smith, a 1983 Kenmore graduate who played football for the Arizona Cardinals, learned to dance at a young age with his mom, who also owned a studio.

"Dominic is just unreal," Smith said. "All the ballet, tap, modern dance and everything he's learned just helps him in soccer and track." Erin Smith said: "Dominic has been with us for seven years and he has natural affinity for dance. Jazz, ballet, modern, hip-hop, jazz, he can do it all."

Sometimes sentiment finds its way into Moore's schedule, too. During a recent practice, Moore worked on a tap duet with his older sister, Nakiasha, who graduated from Firestone. The song was Donna Summer's *Last Dance*.

"We thought it would be a good song to do together since the upcoming contest in Cincinnati will be the last time we dance together," Nakiasha said. An obvious benefit of dance is the physical conditioning it builds.

"I think dancing is more physical than the sports I play," he said. "You use everything dancing and at the end of a hard dance, you can feel every muscle in your body throbbing."

Moore began working dance into his academic studies in middle school at the Miller South School of Visual and Performing Arts. Now he is in the visual and performing arts program at Firestone.

This summer, Moore will attend, on scholarship, a prestigious dance camp in Rochester, N.Y., founded by famed choreographer Garth Fagan, who created the dances for the Broadway musical *Lion King* (1997), winning a Tony Award. One of Fagan's dancers saw Moore perform during a competition and thought he would be perfect for the camp.

"I was shocked they wanted me," Moore said. "Dancing is something I want to do after college, along with playing professional soccer in the MLS (Major League Soccer). I guess all I can say is that I really enjoy all the things that I do and I'm just working hard to get better."

AUTHOR'S INSPIRATION

Dominic was very impressive as a hurdler and I always enjoyed watching him run because of his power, strength and flexibility. I'd have to say that he was a unique hurdler and was one of the best in the state his senior year.

One day, Dominic's coach told me that Dominic has such flexibility and runs with so much grace because he had been taking dance classes since he was a kid. His coach also told me that Dominic was a really, REALLY good dancer, and we're not talking the Homecoming Dance. Dominic was outstanding in modern, jazz, ballet and tap. He also was an All-conference soccer player.

To me, it was a great story to show how versatile Dominic was, and it was important to illustrate to readers how disciplined Dominic was to succeed in everything he did because of his hard work.

CHAPTER 3

HOPE

Bad Actions Forever Alter Young Lives

This is an open letter to students of all ages, especially the African-American males.

Stop acting so tough! Why has it become so easy to settle differences by using violence?

On Tuesday, former City Series football player Anthony Norman Jr. was charged with murder, attempted murder and felonious assault. The case involves a shooting in July that killed an innocent bystander—23-year-old Christopher Harris.

Norman, 19, now at Youngstown State, was arrested on campus Tuesday. The news story was on the front page of the *Beacon Journal*. The same day, a story about another murder appeared on the Local news section. The headline was "Ex-Buchtel star found guilty. Judge sentences man to more than 18 years in prison for Stark murder."

Steve Walker, 20, who was convicted, was another City Series football star, and Norman's high school teammate. Walker, a former University of Pittsburgh player, was found guilty of killing 17-year-old Michael Cheek in July outside a convenience store after an altercation.

These tragic stories should open young people's eyes. Look at what happened and promise to never, ever put yourselves in situations in which the wrong decision could negatively affect you and someone else for the rest of your lives.

For me, the Norman case hits close to home. The past two years, I have been a guest speaker to incoming minority freshmen at my alma mater, Youngstown State. I'm proud of that school and feel honored and privileged every time I'm asked to speak. My topic is always positive, about having fun and taking advantage of this wonderful and exciting time in their lives.

Two years ago, Norman was one of the first people to greet me in the conference hall. He sat right in the front row, listened intently and never took his eyes off me.

Norman was like me when I was a student-athlete at YSU for a short period of time (one of my many mistakes in college ended my baseball career, but it proved to be a valuable life lesson). He seemed excited about starting a new chapter in life. Norman wasn't academically eligible as an incoming freshman, same as I.

Knowing that he was feeling discouraged, I told Norman not to give up, stay strong, keep working hard and that he would be back on the field. When Norman came home on occasion to watch a Griffins football or basketball game, he seemed to be a role model to many of his peers. He represented what each one of them could do if they worked hard in school.

I was proud of Norman.

Now I'm disappointed and disgusted about the alleged actions. I thought he understood the potential danger of that type of violent behavior. Apparently, neither he nor Walker did. They did not appreciate the incredible opportunities that were afforded to them.

Two people's lives were dramatically affected by what happened.

Wait, make that FOUR.

AUTHOR'S INSPIRATION

As a former (black) student-athlete in high school and college and now a professional, I was disappointed to read the stories about two former athletes I covered in high school involved in separate murder cases. It's hard to say they were nice, respectful and good-hearted kids when you read that they were involved in such violent crimes. But the truth is, they were nice, respectful and good-hearted kids . . . AT TIMES. The times they were around professionals, like me, who hoped that they understood the importance of education. But once they were surrounded by their peers, they lacked the discipline—like so many young people, white or black, rich or poor, male or female—to make the right decisions when faced with problematic scenarios.

So many lives were forever altered.

I felt this column needed to be written. It was intended to be a wakeup call to the youth, African-American males specifically, that the greatest asset you can possess is an education. Forget about the knuckleheads who are trying to hold you back because they don't want to see you succeed.

CYO Coach Training Helps Protect Kids: Team Leaders Learn How to Spot Sexual Predators

My good friend, Mike Ede, told me I needed to attend a "meeting" before I could help coach my son's 10th-grade CYO (Catholic Youth Organization) basketball team this year.

Then, my friend said, with glee, "Oh, and Coach Morgan; by the way, it's a three-hour meeting."

Now, I've helped coach my children in CYO in the past and I know there are periodic sessions that coaches are required to attend to learn how to care for athletes who are injured during participation and things of that nature. What I soon found out was that this meeting had nothing to do with how to treat athletes who suffer from minor injuries while playing a sport.

When I arrived at the CYO office, we were taken to a large room, where I was joined by about 20 other coaches from the area. I asked the woman who was leading the meeting, "Excuse me, but what is this meeting all about?"

She called it a "Virtus Training" session and explained it was a three-hour mandatory training session on how to spot signs of inappropriate relations between coaches and CYO athletes. Not what I was expecting at all.

In defense of the CYO, this wasn't a training session in the wake of any inappropriate actions that had been reported. The organization was being proactive in educating the adults who eventually have complete access to young people during the different athletic seasons. For most of my training session, we watched a two-part video of former coaches and/or adult friends of young student-athletes who were convicted of having inappropriate relations with youngsters. Part of the perpetrators' sentencing was to participate in these community-service videos.

Initially, I was disturbed by the frankness of these criminals, who talked so openly about how they manipulated young people, mentally and physically, as coaches or supporters of the young athletes. One man, a girls basketball coach, bragged about how he was able to persuade his players to trust him enough to the point that it was easy to victimize them.

I was angry, appalled and disgusted.

After a while, I understood why I was there for that training session, and I started asking a lot of questions. I realized later that CYO coaches in dioceses all over the country are required to attend this training. The primary reason is to protect the student-athletes.

"I know there is training out there on this subject, but this is a different era than we grew up in," said Don Finn, Akron CYO executive director. "With this training, we're trying to help coaches spot the behavior of sexual predators because there is a pattern."

The training also educated coaches on how to monitor unsupervised access to facilities so that the athletes aren't exposed to individuals who have no business being there. Sure, this is an uncomfortable and sensitive topic, but CYO is doing the right thing. Imagine how a child feels if he or she is or has been a victim and no one recognized and didn't do anything to prevent it.

AUTHOR'S INSPIRATION

Knowing why I had to be at this meeting was somewhat uncomfortable at the beginning. But just a few minutes into the meeting, I soon realized how important it was to be there and to educate myself on the dangers that youngsters face even when it comes to something as nonthreatening as CYO athletics. It was three hours well spent.

White Delivers Christian Message: Former All-Pro Defensive End Leaves Lasting Impression With an Inspired Speech at CVCA

CVCA football player Teddy Harris is a Reggie White fan and not because White is the NFL's all-time sack leader and a future Hall-of-Famer. Harris is a Reggie White fan because of what the former all-pro defensive lineman stands for. "He's a role model to me because he tells you that it's all right to be a Christian," Harris said, following White's

30-minute speech last night at Cuyahoga Valley Christian Academy. White was the guest speaker for "A Night with Reggie White," which was attended by approximately 350 people and included dinner. "He's an inspiration to me," Harris added. "I trust him and I believe in what he believes in."

CVCA coach Ray Carroscia said proceeds from last night's dinner will go to the athletic stadium and the football program. White's son Jeremy was a student last semester at CVCA and his wife, Sara, who grew up in East Cleveland, volunteered in the office once a week. The Whites are living in the area but will be moving to North Carolina in the spring. White, who received a standing ovation from the crowd in the auditorium before he even spoke a word, has been criticized for being so outspoken. In fact, when he addressed the Wisconsin General Assembly last year, some felt his comments were offensive.

"I lost a lot for saying some of the things I did," White said. "I had a $6 million deal with a network and many of my sponsors dropped me so you might say I lost a lot of money. But compared to what God has, it wasn't anything." White is a man who believes in his principles and not public perception, as he said some athletes do. And he had an interesting comment on Atlanta Braves pitcher John Rocker.

"You may not like what John Rocker said but I respect him because he said what a lot of people say in their offices every day, whether you agree with it or not," White said. "I would feel more safe around a guy wearing a hood then around a guy who believes the same thing as John Rocker but I don't know it. People say the Ku Klux Klan are the most dangerous people in America. No they're not. Because you know what they believe," White continued. "The most dangerous people in America are the people who sit in the offices and believe the same thing as the Klan, and they can affect us through the economy."

As White ended his speech, he talked about how important it is for Christians to remain true to their faith. White left a lasting impression on all who heard his message. "His whole outlook on being a Christian is amazing," said 1998 CVCA graduate Kevin Iannetta, who drove from Mount Vernon Nazerene College near Columbus to hear White speak.

AUTHOR'S INSPIRATION

Living in Northeast Ohio with three professional sports teams here, you're bound to run into a Browns, Cavaliers or Indians player at some point. Heck, you may live in the same neighborhood and have a player's kid in your school or classroom.

That was the case with NFL Hall of Famer Reggie White, who had stint with the Cleveland Browns. White, a devout Christian, enrolled his children in Cuyahoga Valley Christian Academy in Cuyahoga Falls, and his wife, Sara worked in the office. No matter how famous White was in regards to his football career, he was always grounded and he always enjoyed speaking to high school students in staying true to their faith at such a crucial time in their lives. He was beloved at CVCA and across the country for being a man of conviction and integrity.

"We were thinking of ways to help the football program in building our stadium when Sara said she and Reggie would love to help out. She suggested that we have Reggie speak at the school as a fundraising dinner," said CVCA athletic director and football coach Ray Carroscia. "Then someone stepped up and paid for the dinner so the entire event was a complete profit. We were able to raise $10,000 that evening. And Reggie gave a strong, faith-based message. He was wonderful."

Reggie White died of a massive heart attack on December 26, 2004, at the age of 43.

CHAPTER 4

REMEMBRANCE

School Tragedy Illustrates Fragility of Life

He loved to play the game of football and to be around his teammates. Friends said he had a warm smile, a sparkle in his eye and a big heart.

And now, 15-year-old Darren Perez is gone.

The Parma Normandy sophomore reserve wide receiver and defensive back died of an aneurysm last Friday. Reports stated that Perez was in the team's weight room Oct. 2 when he collapsed with his teammates—and loyal friends—around him.

He never regained consciousness. How tragic.

Here, a young man leaves his home Thursday morning for school, and no one ever would have imagined that he would not return. The Perez family needs prayers and support.

And when it comes to support from the Normandy football program, it's there, and it comes from one of the most important groups: the Mother's Club, which feeds the players before games and offers loving and sympathetic ears for all the team members, should they need some motherly advice.

Meanwhile, as parents, think about how many times we let our children leave the house without kissing and hugging them. Or telling them we love them. Or not offering up this gentle phrase: "Have a nice day at school," a few words that could be the difference-maker in that child's life for that particular day.

But hey, every family isn't the Brady Bunch or the Huxtables from *The Cosby Show*, right? Sometimes the events that are going on in our lives inadvertently and unknowingly lead us to take people who are close to us for granted, children included. The reality is that there are times when we get too caught up in our own adult worlds that we forget to stay committed to our young ones. That doesn't make us bad parents.

What the Perez tragedy should help us realize is that at the end of the day, it's not about who won the game. It's not about who rushed for 100 yards or scored the most touchdowns or who had the most tackles or kicked the longest field goal.

It's not about neighborhood rivalries getting so nasty to the point that fans are setting bad examples when it comes to sportsmanship. It's about team and love and friendships and camaraderie and families coming together to back each other's kids during the season and cultivating and building friendships that will last long after their children's playing days are over.

Which is why Normandy Athletic Director Harry Caruthers' profound words of wisdom when we spoke on the telephone recently were so gloriously uplifting amid a time of absolute heartbreak. "Through all of this, I think the kids have focused on something special," Caruthers said. "They have focused on the fact that the last thing you say to someone might, in fact, be the very last time that you do say something to them."

Caruthers' point: Never wait to tell someone how much you care about them, because we aren't guaranteed tomorrow. "Unfortunately, our kids had to learn a tough life lesson like this," Caruthers said. "What has helped us is that we have always been a strong team and we're a big family and we wanted to be able to help Darren's family by being here for them.

"To experience what we have gone through in the last week is tough, very tough, but we have bonded together through this tragedy and it's going to help us to move forward."

So knowing that time is not guaranteed, go support your son or daughter in any sport or extracurricular activity. Go watch a neighborhood kid down the street play a sandlot game, and root for him or her.

And lastly, here's a suggestion to high school football sites all across Northeast Ohio tonight. Why not offer a moment of silence once both teams are on the field before the national anthem, not only in honor of Darren Perez, but also in honor of all young men and women who passed away while competing in high school. Because during that moment of silence, maybe we adults will remember to kiss our children goodbye in the morning and whisper to them, "Have a nice day at school."

AUTHOR'S INSPIRATION

I had no idea who Darren Perez was until I opened up the Cleveland Plain Dealer one morning after I returned home from dropping two of my four children off at school. I sat down at my dining room table with a cup of coffee and went to the sports section. I turned the page and there was a mugshot of this All-American looking young man. My initially thought, and I hadn't even read the headlines yet, was "Oh, I wonder what award he won." Then, I read the headline and it blew me away. I felt so bad reading that Darren had passed away at such a young age, with his whole life ahead of him.

The rest of the day, all I thought about was how Darren's parents, family, friends and teammates must have felt. Then I started to think how I would have felt if that tragedy, God forbid, happened to me. I decided to write a column just as a way of telling people (and myself) that we must not take loved ones, especially our children, for granted.

Stringer Played Big on Field, Was Bigger in Life: Stringer Brought Schools and City Together for Title

All you have to do is go back to 1990, Stringer's junior year at Warren G. Harding High School. That was the year the Raiders won the Division I state championship and Stringer was probably the most influential player on that team. Not because of his play on the field, but because of his actions off it.

Prior to the season, Warren Harding and Warren Western Reserve had consolidated. The two perennial powers boasted four state championships between them and had famous alums such as Paul Warfield, Bill Kollar and the Browners—Ross, Jimmy and Joey, all former NFL players. The decision was extremely controversial as most East Siders (the Harding contingent) and West Siders (Reserve) weren't sure what would happen.

But Stringer, just 16 years old at the time, became the ambassador of good will. He brought the entire town together. Blacks. Whites. Italians. Greeks. East Siders. West Siders. Stringer and the Raiders became the biggest story in town.

"I'll never forget that time," said Pete Arnold, who was a member of the Warren Harding Touchdown Club at the time. His son, David, was a former Harding standout who starred at Michigan as a defensive back and played briefly with the Pittsburgh Steelers before returning home to coach Stringer at Harding.

"You still had all kinds of diehards who didn't want to see the two schools come together. There was even tension among the players in the beginning," Arnold said.

Just imagine Canton McKinley and Massillon deciding to consolidate. Or North Canton and GlenOak. St. Vincent-St. Mary and Hoban. Imagine the tug-of-wars. The battle of egos. With the consolidation, that's what you had in Warren, even before the season began.

"We had the kids from both schools in the room and I walked right up to Korey and said, 'Is there going to be any problem with you guys playing together?' Korey stood up and said, 'Don't worry about anything Mr. Arnold, everything is going to be all right.'" And it was. The Raiders won all 14 games, defeating Cincinnati Princeton in the title game.

The way Stringer stood up and took charge then showed the leadership qualities that he carried to Ohio State, where he was an All-American. "Behind closed doors, Korey could be really loose, but other times, he knew when to get tough," said former Ohio State quarterback and current ESPN college football analyst Kirk Herbstreit. "He got along with everybody, whether it was a black player, a white player, a running back or a defensive back. There were no barriers when it came to Korey. He had a way of being a comedian and knocking all of those barriers down."

Former Ohio State coach John Cooper said: "I don't think I ever remember seeing Korey in a bad mood or feeling down and that was a great thing for our football team. He inspired everybody just by the way he carried himself on and off the field. He was such a great leader for us."

University of Akron football coach Lee Owens, the offensive line coach when Stringer was at Ohio State, said he would never forget the time Stringer played St. Nick while the team was in Florida playing in the Citrus Bowl. "Korey dressed in a full Santa Claus outfit and put my kids on his lap," Owens said. "I'll never forget that about him. Korey had the biggest heart."

But even with Stringer's success in college and with the Minnesota Vikings, he never forgot his friends in Warren.

Korey was Korey, polite, well-mannered, respectful. He sent tickets to anyone who would ask him.

Friend Charles Adams remembered one of Stringer's sayings, which was "Just Get Here." That meant, if you could get to a site where Korey would be playing or if he was going to just watch an event, you'd be taken care of while you were with him. "Korey got me on the field for last year's playoff game in Minnesota," Adams said. "And he even hooked us up at the NBA All-Star Game this year. He treated all of us from Warren like he always did, with class and respect."

And Stringer touched the lives of people who barely knew him. Take 48-year-old Jerome Norman. Norman works the third shift at the BP Gas Station on West Market Street in Warren. About a month ago, Stringer pulled into the station for gas. He walked up to the service window, because it was after 11, and asked for gas.

"I knew who Korey Stringer was but I never met him," Norman said. "So when he asked for $20 worth of gas, I said, 'Would you like for me to pump that for you?' I was just being respectful to him because I knew he was a great person."

Stringer's reply? "No way. No way, man. I can get it."

Stringer handed Norman $20 for gas, along with a $50 bill.

Norman, thinking Stringer had accidentally given him too much money, raced out of the store, which now was unattended.

"Mr. Stringer, you gave me too much money."

Stringer turned and said, "No, that's for you brother, you keep that."

That was Korey Stringer, always giving, whether he knew you or not. And as he lay in his coffin yesterday, Stringer, once again, brought the city of Warren together as it paid last respects to a fallen hero.

This is where his heart was.

AUTHOR'S INSPIRATION

Korey's death devastated all of us who knew Korey, watched him grow up in our community and become such a wonderful role model not only as a football player, but also a loving, caring person.

I remember a close friend of mine, Steve Arnold telling me this story. He told me that Korey was home in Warren visiting during the offseason and stopped by the community rec center where he spent a lot of time as a youngster playing basketball. He walked into the gym and said to Steve, "Man, you guys need a new floor and new backboards and hoops." Steve said, "Korey, we just don't have the money to do that." Korey responded, "Get some estimates and I'll pay for it."

Another story that illustrated Korey's kindness and caring towards young athletes occurred when he was at home one year during the off-season. Korey visited one of his former pee-wee football coaches. They talked about what was going on with the team when the coach mentioned that the team was trying to raise money for new uniforms. Korey went into his truck, opened up the glove compartment and took out his check that he had recently received for playing in the Pro Bowl. He endorsed the back of the check, then handed it over to the coach so that the team could buy new uniforms.

Athletes Are Role Models

My role model and hero is John Marsco, who will be 42 in two weeks. John is a longtime friend. He married one of my dear friends from Warren G. Harding High School, the former Debbie Zambelli. John is one of those guys who loves to talk sports. Like me, he grew up memorizing lineups, batting averages, home and away uniform colors of our favorites teams and anything and everything sports related.

The only thing I despise about John (the only thing) is the fact that he is the ultimate Michigan fan. But he's a huge Cavaliers and LeBron James fan. So are his 11-year-old son, Chris, an amazing kid who is just like his dad, and his 7-year-old daughter, Lisa.

The Marsco family got a chance last week to watch the Cavaliers dismantle the Philadelphia 76ers at Quicken Loans Arena. Debbie told me Chris also was a big Cavs and James fan and asked if I would be willing to speak to his fifth-grade class at Cortland Elementary, near my hometown of Warren.

I enjoy speaking to middle- and high-school students about LeBron James and the importance of education. The kids in Mrs. Kristina Denman's class were awesome. At the end of my visit, Debbie asked if I had time to see John. They live a few minutes from the school.

Of course, I agreed. As we pulled into their driveway, I noticed a wheelchair ramp leading to the home's front door. We walked into the house. John was there, happy as a kid on Christmas to see me.

He wasn't the John I remembered, however.

John lay in a hospital bed in his living room. He couldn't move any parts of his body except his head and arms. He could shake my hand and talk to me. That was it.

Two years ago, John was diagnosed with epithelioid sarcoma, a rare form of cancer that attacks bones and soft tissue. The disease is terminal. John receives hospice care.

In late February, John was able to walk. He and Debbie decided they wanted to buy a 42-inch TV. "That was a small investment," said Debbie, who is a younger version of Marion Cunningham from *Happy Days*. That's how sweet she is.

"We decided we wanted to buy a nice TV so we could watch Michigan during the football season." Debbie explained that after they purchased the TV and returned home, ready to assemble the television stand, John walked toward some steps that led upstairs to the bedrooms. He fell. Debbie ran over to help.

"Deb, I'm trying to lift my leg up. I can feel everything, but it won't move," John said. A few days later, doctors discovered John had tumors in his back that eventually paralyzed him from the waist down. He hasn't taken another step since and probably never will.

The ordeal has changed his life and the lives of his family and friends forever. But with everything that has happened to him, John still feels blessed. "David, you know what? Every time I see those little legs come down those steps, every day is a miracle for me."

That's why John, Debbie, Chris and Lisa are my heroes.

AUTHOR'S INSPIRATION

I knew Debbie and John for years. We grew up in the same hometown (Warren) and had been friends for years. Debbie was a huge high school sports fan mainly because of her Dad, Carl, and brothers, Tom and Jimmy, were sports fanatics, especially when it came to the Warren G. Harding Panthers. Debbie's husband, John, was just as fanatic about his alma mater, Warren John F. Kennedy.

John was always helping out the local schools in any way possible—as a scorekeeper, working concession stands or even working the yard sticks on the sideline during football games. So it was sad for me to see John confined to a hospital bed in his home when I visited him and his family. It just didn't seem fair that a caring, loving man in the prime of his life had to go through what he was experiencing. I felt sorry for John, Debbie, Chris and Lisa.

But John showed so much courage and strength, as did his entire family. They didn't feel sorry for themselves. They understood how precious life was so they made sure they took advantage of every second they had together.

John passed away on April 21st, 2004, the day before his 42nd birthday and two years to the day when he was diagnosed with his disease and his family lives off those seconds that they cherished when John was alive.

Tears Flow for Athlete, Julian Long Eulogized as Good Kid

Friends of Julian Long said Friday the 17-year-old had a smile given to him by angels. That's one of the things they'll remember most about the Firestone High senior. His warm, inviting smile seemed to fill everyone's heart.

They'll also remember how Julian, a hard-working student who was well-liked by classmates and faculty, was so full of life and had a promising future. But sorrow filled those hearts Friday afternoon as an estimated 1,000 people—friends, family members, classmates and teammates—gathered at the John S. Knight Center in downtown Akron to pay their last respects to Julian during visiting hours followed by a memorial service.

Julian died a week ago from a rare bacterial infection. He had been a starting defensive end for the Falcons and played in their game a week before his death. Julian also was the City Series track champion in the 110- and 300-meter hurdles last spring as a junior.

"I just can't believe he's gone, I really can't," said Firestone senior Cliff Greer, one of the many close friends Julian had. Cliff also was Julian's football teammate. "I talked to him when he first went into the hospital and he told me how he couldn't wait to get back to the team and that everything was going to be all right. When he passed, it was just a shock and it hurt so much. I still can't handle it," Cliff said. No one could, especially the students. And they came from all over the area.

The Firestone students all hugged and walked together, holding hands and offering support to one another. Race and gender didn't matter. They all shed tears together for a classmate who felt the same way about them.

"Every time Julian would see me, he would say, 'What's up D?' and would give me a hug," said Dior Robinson, a junior at Firestone. "But he would never give you a regular hug. He would always slap your back really hard while he was hugging you. He was a trip. He was a great dude, and I miss him already."

Some students came wearing their varsity jackets. All eight schools from the City Series were represented. There were visitors with jackets from Copley and Canton McKinley, too. Kenmore High's Matt Kirksey said, "I didn't go to school with Julian but I knew him from playing sports against him and I just had to come here and pay my respects." Matt, a star running back for the Cardinals, also wore his varsity jacket. "I just had to come," he said. "This is just . . . sad."

Jasmina Nolan, a cheerleader at Garfield, went to middle school with Julian at Litchfield in Akron. She also was wearing her varsity jacket. As Jasmina and a group of friends were leaving the service, they said they felt blessed and privileged for the opportunity to have known Julian.

"This just goes to show you how much Julian meant to all of us," she said. "Julian was the kind of person who would do anything for you." Classmate Jennifer Flakes recalled a time when Julian helped her, Jasmina and Shamoriea Hilliard out when they were in a jam. But they said Julian helped them out in his own unique way, which made him such a good person. "We were at the St. Sebastian Festival and our car wouldn't start," Jennifer said. "We needed someone to help us, so Julian came over, got under the hood and helped us jump-start our car. But right before he got it going, he started jumping and flipping around like he was electrocuted. He just started laughing and after a few seconds, we did, too. That's how he was, always having fun."

St. Vincent-St. Mary football coach Jay Brophy was one of many area coaches who attended the service with some of their players. Tramontay McWain and Justin Walker accompanied Brophy. "A lot of our guys wanted to come, but they just couldn't do it," Brophy said.

One Irish player who didn't go was senior Sian Cotton. "I really wanted to go but I knew Julian and I knew I just wasn't going to be able to handle it," he said. Brophy said the tragedy hit his team hard because many of his players knew Julian. The Irish defeated Firestone earlier this year. "Something like this—so tragic—destroys you," Brophy said. "We said a prayer for Julian at Mass."

Brophy said Julian's death took him back to a tragic time in his life. Brophy was a teammate of All-City basketball player Wayne Johnson, a Buchtel star who collapsed and died on the court at Warren G. Harding

High in the mid-1970s during a game. "I can understand how Julian's teammates feel," Brophy said. "It's been 25 years since Wayne died and I still live with that. It's devastating."

But the love the students showed toward Julian yesterday was amazing. "We just have to keep Julian's spirit alive," said one student, who was having trouble keeping her composure as she spoke, and didn't want to be identified. "We're all here because we all loved Julian so much and we just feel really, really bad that he died so young.

"We're going to miss him so much but deep in our hearts we know he's going to a better place. Keep on smiling, Julian."

AUTHOR'S INSPIRATION

I was driving to Ypsilanti, Mich., on a Saturday morning to cover a football game between the University of Akron and Eastern Michigan when I received a telephone call on my cell phone from a student at Firestone who was a friend and teammate of Julian. He said, "Hello, Mr. Morgan. I was just calling to tell you that we all left the hospital and it looks like Julian isn't going to make it." First of all, I was absolutely blindsided because I had no idea there was anything wrong with Julian. I had known the young man for several years and he was one of the nicest, friendliest kids you'd ever meet. In fact, he had played in a football game the night before. The student who called me said Julian had some rare illness that hit him quickly. Unfortunately, Julian died a few days later. I covered the funeral and I have to say that it was probably one of the saddest moments of my life. It was like losing a family member.

Buchtel High Coach Dies During Surgery: Community Mourns Ed Ponder, 45, Who Was Inspiration to Players

The Buchtel High School community is mourning the loss of a man who was called "an inspiration." Girls basketball coach Ed Ponder, 45, died yesterday of complications that occurred during coronary bypass surgery at Akron General Medical Center. "From what I understand, one of Eddie's arteries just kept bleeding and bleeding and the doctors couldn't stop it," said one of Mr. Ponder's closest friends, Harvey Sims, the former boys basketball coach at Buchtel.

Mr. Ponder's death has "ripped me apart," Sims said. "I was in town last week for a wrestling tournament and Eddie called me and asked me to come to a party he was having Saturday at his house because he was having surgery. But I couldn't make it and I feel bad that I couldn't go.

"Maybe he knew something we didn't know and that was his way of getting people together," Sims said, struggling to keep his composure.

Mr. Ponder is survived by his wife, Gisele, who works at Akron General, and daughters Nicole, a student at the University of Akron, and Courtney, a sophomore at Buchtel and a member of the girls basketball team.

Longtime Buchtel track coach John Scott coached Mr. Ponder's daughters. "I've known Eddie for six years and I can honestly say that I felt like I've known him all my life," Scott said. "He and I became such good friends, and when you have a friend that close to you pass away, it's like losing a sibling."

Scott attended Mr. Ponder's party Saturday and said the family always wanted visitors to feel welcome and have a good time. "We danced and played music all night long," Scott said. "It was a fun time and we all expected Eddie to come out of this. It just goes to show you that life and friendships are precious."

Friends said Mr. Ponder reinvented himself after battling cancer and undergoing triple bypass surgery several years ago. He took early retirement from the Akron Fire Department and became a teacher at Buchtel. After serving as an assistant coach under Sims and helping on the football staff, Mr. Ponder finally got the chance to become a head coach, taking over the girls program this season.

Mr. Ponder led the Griffins to this year's City Series championship game, where the Griffins lost to Firestone 56-53 in double overtime. "How couldn't you respect a man like Eddie?" Firestone coach Audley McGill said. "He was a classy guy who just wanted to see all of his kids succeed."

Mr. Ponder never liked to draw attention to himself. He showed up for work Monday, the day before the surgery. "He looked very pale and his face was drawn, and I said to him, 'Eddie, are you going to be OK?' " secretary Carol Beasley said. "He said, 'I was worried, but now that I'm in school, I feel a lot better.' He told me (the surgery) would be no big deal and that he didn't want any flowers or fruit baskets sent to him.

"He said he would be out for about a month and he would be back. That was Eddie. He was always low-key, a kind gentleman who was a family man, believed in God, was active in his church and always wanted to give back to the community."

Buchtel athletics director Yvonne Hume said there was an eerie silence in the school hallways following the announcement of Mr. Ponder's death. "We told the students that they could come down to the auditorium if they needed support or just wanted to talk," Hume said. "Everybody left the classrooms, but it was really quiet. All you could hear was soft crying. Kids were in the hallways hugging each other. They knew Eddie was always there for anyone, not just his daughters."

Buchtel sophomore guard Jasmin Flinn, a first-team All-City Series player, was stunned by the news. "I just can't believe he's gone," Flinn said. "But I believe in my heart that he's coaching in a better place." Flinn remembers the times Mr. Ponder would pick players up for practices or a game if they didn't have rides. And if they wanted to go to other games around town, Mr. Ponder would take them all, as a team.

"He loved everybody," Flinn said.

Teammate Tasha Terrell said Mr. Ponder would always go beyond the call of duty. "He was a father figure to most of the players," she said. "He was always telling jokes in practice just to keep us laughing. When we had practices in the morning, he would bring us doughnuts if we hadn't eaten yet.

"But the biggest thing I remember about him is last week, he saw me walking in the hallway between classes and he said, 'Come here, girl, and give me a hug.' He cared."

Buchtel football coach Claude Brown said, "I loved Eddie as a man because of what he meant to Buchtel. He didn't have to be here after his disability but he wanted to teach the kids and give them some direction in their lives."

AUTHOR'S INSPIRATION

Eddie was one of those gentlemen in the community who always wanted to see you reach your full potential in everything you did. He was such a great role model for young men and women in the black community and to lose him so suddenly was mindboggling. At the same time, his death was a call to action for those in the Buchtel community and for others who knew him to continue their quest for reaching their full potential, in his honor.

Area Youth Leader Dies at Age of 70: Anderson Was Coach, Father Figure to Many Youngsters in Akron

Walter Anderson loved young people, loved watching them succeed in sports and in life, and was a father figure to so many in the Akron community. In fact, while Anderson was coaching neighborhood kids and young adults in the Akron recreation leagues, friends and family said the 70-year-old was known to have a basketball in one hand and a Bible in the other.

And when Anderson is laid to rest today, he'll be buried the same way—with a basketball in one hand and a Bible in the other. Anderson, 70, passed away at his home Friday due to an extended illness.

"Walter will have a Bible in his hand, and somehow, we're going to get a basketball in there, too," Anderson's widow, Berlene, said as she laughed.

Anderson, a 1950 graduate of South High School, made a commitment to the youth in the area and never wavered. He was a coach, a companion and a caring person, but as one friend said, more than anything, Anderson was a Christian.

"That man was a true humanitarian," said Roger Moore, who is a former recreation department and children's services worker. "Wherever he is, I know he's with the Father, because he definitely cared about his fellow man."

Anderson and his wife of more than 40 years raised five children (four boys and a girl), and they have 20 grandchildren and six great-grandchildren. Berlene is saddened by the loss, but her heart swelled and her words resonated with pride as she spoke about her husband.

"He never met a stranger in his life because everyone he met became his friend," she said. "He was kind to everyone and he always had something positive to say about everybody."

For more than 40 years, Anderson was active in various church, civic and sports organizations and would always be willing to help in any way he could. James "Vito" Davis is a recreation department volunteer who coaches youth sports year-round. He was one of Anderson's former basketball players, and the reason he became a volunteer is because he wanted to follow in Anderson's footsteps.

"Mr. Anderson cared about every kid he came in contact with," Davis said. "And if you were a coach, and you needed a sponsor, he would get you a sponsor. That's because people in the community—black and white—respected him as a man. I'm coaching because I feel like I have to give back to the community like he did."

One of the Anderson's sons, Phillip, said he is proud of the legacy his father has left behind. "He touched so many people and not just in sports," Phillip said. "He was a Christian and a good man, and he taught you that there was more to life than just sports. But he loved sports, and he loved the Lord."

AUTHOR'S INSPIRATION

I didn't know Mr. Anderson well, but what I did know was that he was a man that every community had and that every community needed. He was always about what was best for the kids in the neighborhood. But what made him even more special was that it didn't matter if you were from his neighborhood or not. He was always willing to help anyone in need, no matter where they came from.

East Lineman Dies at Akron Hospital: Aunt Says Jonte' Hightower's Blood Sugar Too High

2007 was going to be Jonte' Hightower's year. He was looking forward to finishing his senior year at East High School, then continuing his football career next season at Hudson Valley Community College in Troy, N.Y. But his young life ended suddenly Tuesday morning. An autopsy is scheduled to determine a cause of death.

Hightower just celebrated his 18th birthday—on Christmas Day. "We were all so excited about Christmas and the New Year because Jonte' was excited about his future," said Hightower's aunt, Dierdre Dulaney. "He felt like he was on the verge of making something of himself. He couldn't wait to go to college and play football. That's what's so hard about this whole thing. He was so vibrant."

Dulaney said her nephew, who was 6-foot-2, 360 pounds and was a starting offensive lineman for East this past season, spent the night at a friend's house on Sunday when he complained of feeling ill. Hightower's condition was bad enough that he was taken to Akron Children's Hospital on Monday afternoon. "Jonte' was feeling weak at his friend's house so they took him to the hospital," Dulaney said. "When he got there, he was disoriented, his speech was slurring and he could hardly walk." Dulaney said once her nephew was admitted to the hospital, his condition deteriorated. His blood sugar was tested and it was dangerously high. Dulaney said it was at 2,000. A normal blood sugar reading is between 70 and 120. "That's the thing, he never had any signs that he was diabetic," Dulaney said.

Hightower couldn't be stabilized once he was in the hospital. His organs started to fail and he died. "The crazy part is that his mother died when she was 19 and Jonte' was just 18 months old," said Dennis Cox, who coached Hightower at Central-Hower High School for two years, before Hightower transferred to East after Central-Hower closed.

"He was like a son to me, that's what's so devastating," Cox said. "It's so sad. I can't believe it. It's like I'm dreaming." East football coach Damon Beasley said "I just saw Jonte' at our annual banquet at the end of the year a few weeks ago, and he was our co-Offensive Lineman of the Year. He worked so hard all year to get better so that he could play in college. I feel terrible for that whole family."

AUTHOR'S INSPIRATION

This was another sad, tragic story that I hated to write. It always seems so unfair when you see a young athlete's life cut short. But what Hightower's family did was use their loss to help others become aware of the dangers of high blood sugar in juveniles.

The Heart of the Matter: His Late Sister Still Inspires McKinley's Hall

Antonio Hall has a heart as big as his physique—and he's 6-foot-5, 305 pounds. The Canton McKinley senior lineman is one of the best in the state at his position. Actually, he's ranked as one of the best in the nation. But the accolades don't mean much to Hall.

Don't get the wrong idea. He's grateful and honored for all the preseason attention he's been receiving. But he knows how to keep it all in perspective. A recent traumatic experience in Hall's life has made him look at things differently. And his sister, Erica Moore, helped Hall stay grounded.

Moore died of cancer in December at age 15. She was very close to Hall. They were about as tight as any brother and sister could be. If you look at Hall's left arm, you'll see a tattoo in her honor. It reads "One love, Lil Sis."

"She was my heart," said Hall, who was very emotional talking about the loss of Erica. "She was a strong person. I miss her every day." It is such a contrast—watching Hall knock around players during practice like rag dolls, then sitting down a few minutes later after practice and listening to his soft-spoken voice break up as he talks about Erica.

"She was my heart," Hall said once again.

Hall said he understands that life includes adversity, and overcoming those obstacles makes everyone stronger."I live my life through the Lord and he has blessed me with my ability to play football," Hall said. "And I believe that everything happens for a reason. Sometimes the Lord is testing us and you have to accept what happens and become stronger from your experiences."

Hall seems to have decided that what happened in his life can help him to lead others by example—both on and off the football field. And so McKinley couldn't ask for a better leader.

Hall is in his third season as a starter, and he knows what's expected of a senior captain. He was a member of McKinley's back-to-back Division I state championship teams in 1997 and 1998. The experience he has gained has been invaluable.

"Playing with guys like Kenny Peterson, Jamar Martin and Mike Doss (all playing at Ohio State), you learn what you have to do to lead the team," Hall said. "I understand it's my turn to be the leader and everything I've been through has prepared me for this year."

And Hall has the respect from his teammates and coaches. "Antonio is a very hard worker and he helps you want to work just as hard as he does," said Garrett Bush, a 6-4, 270-pound lineman who is also being heavily recruited by Division I schools. "We all look up to Antonio like a big brother."

McKinley head coach Kerry Hodakievic said: "Antonio is everything you want in a team leader. He has the physical ability but he also has the right frame of mind. He's a good kid. Anyone would be happy to have a guy like him on their team."

Hall said Erica inspired him to love life and not take things for granted. She also has enabled him to become a stronger person. "I know whatever I go through on the football field and in school or wherever else, it can't be nearly as bad as what Erica went through," Hall said. "She's my heart."

AUTHOR'S INSPIRATION

The game of football is a rough and tough sport where guys beat and mangle one another's bodies for hours. And there's no crying. But don't tell that to Antonio, this oversized-teddy-bear-of-a-lineman. He lost his sister just before the start of the season his senior year and it was hard to get himself back together for the season. He was an emotional wreck. But knowing that his sister's name was etched forever on his arm was comforting.

Baseball Player Steps Up in Crisis: North Olmsted Woman Sees UA Student as Hero for Efforts to Aid Spouse

Being a hero isn't always about scoring a touchdown or hitting a home run. Being a hero is about caring for people.

Doing what's right. Trying to save a life.

In Marge Gotro's eyes, Ben McCauley is a hero. McCauley, a former standout baseball player for Triway and a senior pitcher for the University of Akron Zips, met Gotro under the most tragic circumstances imaginable. McCauley and the Zips were in Marietta for a baseball game against Ohio University. Gotro and her husband, Doug, also were in Marietta last weekend. The couple of 48 years were headed back to their home in North Olmsted after a golfing trip to Fort Myers, Fla. They had stopped at the Holiday Inn.

"We always stop in Marietta because it's a four-hour drive from Cleveland," Gotro said. "My husband and I had a delightful dinner and we went to our rooms. I took a shower and went to bed. Doug took a shower, but when he got out, he just dropped to the floor."

Gotro said her husband had a history of congestive heart problems, but she thought he had just bumped into the coffee table and fallen.

It was more serious than that.

"I ran over to him to see if he was all right, but he was sweating heavily. I knew right then something was seriously wrong," she said.

Gotro called 911, and just as she hung up the telephone and opened the door to yell for help, McCauley and Zips teammate Chris Maczko, a former Barberton standout, were walking down the hall. McCauley had just pitched nine innings in a victory over the Ohio University Bobcats. However, he would soon realize that the baseball game didn't mean a thing with a man's life hanging in the balance.

"As soon as we passed the door, (Gotro) said, 'My husband has fallen down. Do you guys think you can help me, please?' " McCauley said.

The two players went into the room and knew immediately it was a critical situation.

Maczko ran to the front desk for help. He passed McCauley's father, Robert, who found out what was happening and went to assist his son. They both are trained in CPR. "The one young man (Ben McCauley) was over top of my husband and saying, 'Doug. Doug. Hang in there, guy.

We're going to get you through this,'" Gotro said. "I went out in the hallway and there were people coming from their rooms. We just stood in the hallway and prayed. It's unbelievable how the American spirit works."

Robert McCauley was vigorously performing chest compressions while his son was administering mouth-to-mouth resuscitation.

"I wasn't really nervous. I was just doing what I could," Ben McCauley said. "When I went in the room, the man was breathing sporadically and I got a pulse on the carotid artery. There were five or 10 seconds between each pulse."

Meanwhile, Holly Davis, a Holiday Inn worker on duty that evening, also tried to help resuscitate Gotro. Davis was feeling for a pulse as well, which she said was faint. When the paramedics arrived, they were surprised to see how well the group was working together in the life-saving attempt.

"They told us that we were doing great and to continue performing CPR while they got set up," Robert McCauley said. Gotro was transported to a nearby hospital, but died of cardiac arrest. He was 73. The funeral will be held Friday at the Church of St. Luke the Evangelist in suburban Lakewood.

"When it was all said and done, I completely fell apart," Davis said. "Ben's mother (Cindy) really took care of me." Marge Gotro said it was Davis who gave her support after her husband was transported to the hospital.

"But Ben was an angel," said Davis, who had never met McCauley until that evening. "His family and his friend (Maczko) were amazing. All I can say is that they are all angels."

Ben McCauley said he learned a valuable lesson that night. A lesson he'll keep with him the rest of his life. "I think God has a way of making me feel thankful for everything I have, and this was his way," McCauley said. "It just goes to show you that you never know when your life can be taken from you."

Marge Gotro agreed. "We had no warning at all that this was going to happen," she said. "But I really want to thank the young men who helped me, especially Ben. He was right with it the whole time. There are so many wonderful young people in the world.

"Ben treated Doug like he was his grandfather. He was so gentle, yet intense. I looked for (Ben) the next day, but I guess the team had left. If I ever see him again, I would just give him a big hug and thank him for everything he did."

AUTHOR'S INSPIRATION

This was one of those stories that just moves you when you read the details. People stepping up in crisis to help their fellow Americans, whether you know them or not. The same sense of compassion and caring we saw during the tragedy that took place on 9/11.

CHAPTER 5

LEBRON'S LEGACY

Irish Star Keeps It in Perspective: Freshman James Hears the Hype, but Main Goal Is to Help Team Win Title

Imagine how mature a kid like St. Vincent-St. Mary's LeBron James must be to handle all the hype.

The 6-foot-4 guard just turned 15 and already the expectations surrounding him are high. But if you've seen James' fluid moves and sweet jump shot, you'd understand why. James, a second-team Division III All-Ohioan, is arguably one of the best high school freshman basketball players in the state. And some in the Irish camp will argue that he's one of the best freshman in the country.

James leads the Irish in scoring (17.7 points a game), rebounds (5.92), assists (3.56), steals (3.16) and blocked shots (22), and you're talking about a team that is 25-0, ranked No. 21 nationally by *USA Today* and is two games away from claiming a Division III state championship.

"I knew he was an awfully good player and I guess it became a question as to whether he's the best freshman in the area, the best in the state or even the best in the country," said St. V-M coach Keith Dambrot. "I knew he would be one of the best (freshmen) in the state, but until I started coaching him, I didn't realize how much better he was going to get."

Villa Angela-St. Joseph longtime coach Tedd Kwasniak said James is on the same level as some current NBA players when they were in high school.

"LeBron is the same caliber of player that Stephon Marbury, Cherokee Parks and Danny Ferry (Cavs) were in high school and we played against those kids," said Kwasniak, who also worked at VASJ when former NBA star Clark Kellogg was there. "I can see LeBron being an outstanding Big Ten, ACC-type college player."

After the Irish defeated VASJ 58-51 Saturday to advance to Friday's state semifinal game in Columbus against Canal Winchester (24-1), Kwasniak even said James could be a future NBA player as long as he continues to work hard.

See what James has to deal with? The comparisons. The high expectations. The hype. But that's when James' maturity surfaces and he puts everything into perspective.

"I'm only a freshman," he said. "I'm only worried about getting to the state championship game and getting through my ninth-grade year.

"Sometimes I do think about what I'll be doing in the future and I'd like to go to college and someday play in the NBA," he continued. "But right now, I want to concentrate on high school and keep working hard to develop my skills. I love playing here and I love my teammates. We are like a family."

Dambrot said James does a great job of balancing the pressures of being one of the leaders on an undefeated and nationally ranked team with being just a regular high school freshman.

"LeBron has the unique ability to know when to have fun, when to be loose and when it's time to get down to business," Dambrot said.

"He'll be the funny man before practice but as soon as practice starts, he turns it on. He's a very mature basketball player who loves the game."

Before practice yesterday, Kevin Molinelli, a seven-year-old first-grader at St. Sebastian School, was at St. Vincent-St. Mary with his mom, Patti Molinelli. Kevin was introduced to James and after the two shook hands, Kevin walked away with a smile on his face as if he had just met Michael Jordan.

"He was so excited," Patti Molinelli said. "That made his day because Kevin really likes LeBron. That's all he talked about on the way home."

James seems to have reached star status in some circles, yet his head isn't in the clouds. He meets and greets everyone with an innocent smile.

"And when LeBron comes home, he's just my 15-year-old son," said Gloria James. "I still have to get on him about things like making his bed."

Make the key pass . . . make the winning basket . . . make the bed. Hmm, that could be one reason LeBron James is able to remain focused on the task at hand.

AUTHOR'S INSPIRATION

When I started covering LeBron as a freshman, the first thing I noticed was how mature he was as a 14-year-old. I mean, he was goofy, big-earred LeBron off the court, but on the court, he was as serious as a fifth-year senior in college. I saw that maturity at an early age and it was something that tipped me off. I knew there was something special and unique about LeBron and that I would have to watch him and keep him on my radar.

Invincible Irish: Joyce, James Lift Unbeaten St. V-M to Div. III Title

The 13,061 fans at Value City Arena who watched St. Vincent-St. Mary against Jamestown Greeneview in the Division III boys state title game witnessed the most inspirational story of the tournament.

It was the story of a 5-foot-3, 95-pound freshman guard named Dru Joyce from St. V-M. In a game where height usually matters, Joyce never has let his lack of height discourage him. And in the most important game of his young career, Joyce's performance was monumental.

Joyce, who turned 15 in January, came off the bench and made 7-of-7 3-pointers, one shy of the state tournament record in Division III, and finished with 21 points, as the Irish defeated Jamestown Greeneview 73-55 to win their first state title since 1984. St. V-M (27-0) also finished the year as the state's only unbeaten team. "This is an amazing feeling," the soft-spoken Joyce said. "I never expected anything like this."

Neither did Greeneview. "Other than (LeBron) James, I felt we did a nice job on the other two guys (Maverick Carter and Aly Samabaly)," Greeneview coach Bill Green said. "But I didn't expect a kid like (Joyce) to step up like he did. That was the difference."

James led the Irish with 25 points and nine rebounds.

Once the game ended, Joyce found himself in an unfamiliar position, being surrounded by television cameras. After his on-court interviews, Joyce was hoisted into the air by his teammates, as St. V-M fans cheered "Druuuuuuu." He had to feel 10 feet tall.

St. V-M coach Keith Dambrot never has hesitated to use Joyce. Dambrot knows what he's getting when Joyce is on the court: an intelligent player who works hard on defense and can shoot. Boy, can he shoot. "I knew Dru was a player the first time I saw him," Dambrot said. "Watching him have a game like this is just a great feeling. He's like me; we're the guys who don't get picked on the playground. I can't tell you how happy I am for Dru."

"I'm a proud dad," said Dru Joyce Sr., an assistant coach for the Irish. "Dru is a small player, so there are times when he won't get many looks at the basket, but for a while there, they (Greeneview) packed their defense in and kind of dared Dru to shoot. He picked a great day to find his rhythm."

Dru Joyce said he was "unconscious" after he made his first few 3-pointers, and his dad said he could tell it was going to be a good day for his son. "He kept calling for the ball, and that was a good sign," Dru Joyce Sr. said.

St. V-M senior Maverick Carter was smart enough to know who had the hot hand. On Friday night, it was Carter who had the shooting touch. He led the Irish with 26 points on 10-of-13 shooting. However, yesterday, Carter didn't have the touch, scoring six points (2-of-8). But when Carter was running the offense, he knew to find Joyce.

"We have the type of team where guys can create shots for one another," Carter said. "When I saw Dru was feeling good, I started penetrating more so the defense would pick me up; then I would just kick it out to Dru, and he came through for us."

Greeneview guard Gregg Haines (17 points) said he was impressed with Joyce. "We kept tying to go out on him and put a hand in his face, but he always seemed to get his shot off," Haines said.

When Joyce enters a game, he knows opponents won't give him much respect. He said he's had opponents ask him if he's in the fifth grade or if he's hit puberty yet.

"I know what I can do on the court," Joyce said. "I don't let any of that stuff get to me. I just worry about doing my job."

Greeneview (23-5) put together a very effective game plan, which consisted of playing a zone defense and forcing the Irish to make their shots from the perimeter. The Irish did.

At the end of the first quarter, the game was tied at 17, and at halftime, St. V-M led 30-27. But the Irish pushed the lead to 48-35 late in the third quarter on back-to-back 3-pointers by Joyce. However, Joyce's biggest 3-pointer was his shot at the buzzer, which gave St. V-M a 17-point lead (55-38).

AUTHOR'S INSPIRATION

Think about this for a moment. You're LeBron James, Dru Joyce, Willie McGee and Sian Cotton. You guys are only freshmen, scrawny, not-yet-developed freshmen, mentally, or physically, you're a Division III team but you played Division I teams all year long, and with all of those challenges, you not only won the state championship, you were never beaten in 27 games.

That's what amazed me the most about LeBron and this squad. In fact, as much as LeBron and his buddies wanted to win a high school national championship, which they did their senior year, to me their freshmen year was the most impressive display of handling grace under pressure.

This Little Guy's a Big Shot: Although Only 5-5, Dru Joyce Jr.'s Long-Range Bombs Key Factor in Irish Offense

The day after St. Vincent-St. Mary defeated Jamestown Greeneview 73-55 to win the Division III state title last year, the Joyce family was dining at a local restaurant. A server at the restaurant brought seven balloons to the table and tied each one of them to the arm of Dru Joyce Jr.

The balloons represented the seven 3-point shots Joyce made during one of the most impressive individual performances in the history of the state tournament. Joyce was 7-of-7 from 3-point range for 21 points and was one long-range basket short of tying the Division III record for most 3-pointers in a championship game.

"That game was exciting and unbelievable for me," said Joyce, who is back—at 5-5 this year—in the state title game this year as the Irish (25-1) play Miami East (25-2) at 11 A.M. today. "After I made my first few shots, I felt like I couldn't miss. I guess it's that shooter's mentality. Once you hit a few shots and get on a roll, you start to believe you can hit them all."

What made Joyce's performance so spectacular is that he was a 5-foot-3 freshman at the time and the crowd of 13,061 at Ohio State's

Schottenstein Center adopted him as its hero. Every time Joyce threw up a shot, the crowd would yell "Druuuu" in anticipation of yet another successful 3-pointer by Joyce. He became a symbol of hope and determination. "I had people come up to us long after that game and tell me their sons and daughters had Dru's picture up on their bedroom walls," said Dru Joyce Sr., an assistant coach for the Irish. "They said he was an inspiration for all the little people."

Dru Jr.'s performance definitely was an inspiration to St. V-M coach Keith Dambrot, who isn't much taller than Joyce. Dambrot said he has a special relationship with Joyce. "I was really happy for him. I mean every day, the little guys always have to prove that they belong," Dambrot said. "All year long, people said Dru was playing just because his dad was a coach or they would say I was stupid for playing him. Dru's game was kind of like redemption. He showed people the type of player he was and how much heart he has."

Assistant coach Lee Cotton, who, along with Dru Sr., has coached Joyce on their AAU teams since he was nine, said he knew Dru had the ability to have such a spectacular game. "I thought it was really amazing but I never thought it was out of his capability," said Cotton, father of sophomore forward Sian and senior guard Lee Jr. "I've seen Dru hit four or five (3-pointers) in a row so it didn't surprise me that he made seven. I was surprised that he did it in such a big game and being just a freshman."

The Joyces have a videotape of Dru's game but the sophomore said he doesn't watch it very often. "Once in a while, I'll throw the tape in but, once the season started, I tried to focus on this year," he said. "I was just concerned with us getting get back to the state championship game." On the other hand, Dru Joyce Sr. and his wife Carolyn and their younger son Cameron, never hesitate to watch Dru Jr.'s outstanding game.

"We had some relatives over the house recently who didn't go to the championship game last year and we showed it to them," Dru Sr. said. "We even showed it to some of our relatives from out of town at Thanksgiving. They were all impressed."

As were the fans at Schottenstein Center.

AUTHOR'S INSPIRATION

I tell this story all the time when I speak at schools across the state and they ask about LeBron and his high school teammates. I tell the story about how Little Dru got no respect from opponents his freshman year game, after game, after game.

When Little Dru walked onto the court for a game, he was so little and his game shorts were so big that it looked like he was wearing sweatpants. Boy, how deceiving. Little Dru was tough as nails and could hold his own on any court, with any opponent, on any given night. In this state championship game, Little Dru made Value City Arena his stage—his coming out party—and there were 13,061 guests.

St. V-M Nearly Reaches Summit: James Scores 33, but Irish Fall to Oak Hill 79-78

It was tough for St. Vincent-St. Mary to keep its emotions in check after last night's 79-78 loss to Oak Hill Academy, the No. 1 team in the country. Irish sophomore forward LeBron James wanted to win this game more than anything. So did his teammates. A win for the Irish (9-1), ranked No. 3 in the country, probably would've made them the top team in the nation.

But when James' last-second running jumper rolled around the rim and bounced out as the final buzzer sounded during the National Hoops Classic at Battelle Hall, St. V-M and its fans were crushed. That's when James, who scored a game-high 33 points, let his tears flow.

"I'm proud of everybody, the players, the coaches, the fans. . . . We had a chance to win, but the shot just wouldn't go in," James said. "It hurts, but we got all the tears and frustration and disappointment out of our system, and now, it's time to get back to work."

"I feel really bad for LeBron," St. V-M coach Keith Dambrot said. "He played a great game. Everything we did was because of him. Don't get me wrong, everyone played well, but LeBron was outstanding."

And he's just 15, which impresses Oak Hill coach Steve Smith, whose team is 18-0.

"(LeBron) plays with a lot of confidence, and he had us on our heels all night," Smith said. "If he's a senior, he's an All-American."

The Irish had other quality performances.

Sophomore guard Dru Joyce, all 5-foot-3 of him, scored 15 points on 5-of-5 shooting from behind the 3-point line. In St. V-M's state championship win last year, Joyce was 7-of-7 from long range.

Aly Samabaly (nine points) and John Taylor (eight points) hit some key shots and played strong defense.

Romeo Travis (nine points, seven rebounds) and Sian Cotton were undersized but battled underneath while Jermeny Johnson and Willie McGee did what they could off the bench. It was a team effort that kept St. V-M ahead for most of the game.

The Irish weren't intimidated at all by Oak Hill's squad, which features several Division I college recruits, including Billy Edelin (Syracuse), Rashaad Carruth (Kentucky) and a 7-foot senior center named De Sagana Diop, who will be playing major college basketball next year.

Edelin scored 29 points and was 12-of-12 from the field, Carruth added 19, and Diop had 15.

"We didn't come down here for a moral victory," Dambrot said. "We came down here to win. Our kids weren't intimated, and they weren't scared. They came ready to play."

St. V-M led 19-18 after the first quarter, 42-36 at halftime and, in the early minutes of the third quarter, led 52-42. But the Warriors backcourt duo of Edelin and Carruth helped Oak Hill take a 62-60 lead heading into the fourth quarter.

The lead changed eight times in the final quarter, and the Irish led 78-77 with 1:50 left. James had two chances to extend the lead but missed the front-end of two one-and-ones. The Warriors took advantage, and Edelin's layup with 1:35 left was the game-winner. "We played smart, we played hard and we had a chance to win," Dambrot said. "This is a great group of kids."

AUTHOR'S INSPIRATION

I remember this game well. I was covering the game in Columbus and it was a surreal atmosphere. Oak Hill was this perennial national power that produced numerous high-profile Division I college recruits, not to mention future first-round NBA picks. And here was St. Vincent-St. Mary, a small, private school from Akron.

On paper, it appeared that the Irish would be outmatched, but they weren't. LeBron led his team right down to the wire and his last-second shot, which rolled in and out of the rim, was the difference. I had never seen LeBron ever get emotional after a loss, but this was the first—and only—time I saw him cry after a loss. The truth was that LeBron and his teammates showed the rest of the country that St. V-M was a team that was for real and a team to be reckoned with on a national level for the next few seasons.

St. V-M: Things You Didn't Know (and Didn't Think to Ask): Taylor Talks to the Mirror, Cotton Writes Poetry and Travis Likes to Sleep

Ann Garber, director of development at St. Vincent-St. Mary, and Patty Burdon, director of adsmissions, came up with a clever idea.

They figured that people know about the success of the boys basketball team—that the Irish, the defending Division III state champs, are 24-1, ranked No. 1 in the state and No. 4 in the country and will be playing in the state semifinals Thursday in Columbus against Wayne Trace.

"But we want people to know them for more than just basketball," Garber said. So, with the help of Garber and Burdon, here are some things you might not have known about the players (in alphabetical order):

- Jamie Cavileer, junior guard—Carries a 3.3 grade-point average, loves rap music and said that the funniest thing he's experienced since being on the team is listening to teammate LeBron James sing on the bus.

- Josh Cavileer, junior guard and cousin of Jamie—His favorite movie is *For Love of the Game*. His funniest moments on the team: "When (teammate) John Taylor looks in the mirror before a game and asks, 'Why am I so pretty,' and watching Aly (Samabaly) trying to make jokes but is at a loss for words." Samabaly was born in Zaire.
- Sian Cotton, sophomore forward—He is known for his physical style of play inside but his hobby is writing poetry. "Serious poetry," he said. He's been writing poetry for six years. His brother, Lee Jr., is on the team, and his father, Lee Sr., is an assistant coach.
- Lee Cotton, senior forward/guard—He hopes to be an athletic trainer, and said that he has learned the value of friendships and teamwork during his career at St. V-M.
- LeBron James, sophomore guard—He's a candidate for Mr. Basketball in Ohio, which goes to the best player in the state. His career choice is to play in the NBA, then become a radio announcer. He carries a 2.8 GPA.
- Jermeny Johnson, junior center—He wants to be an engineer, and said that the funniest thing that has happened to him was when "I got spaghetti legs and lost the ball."
- Dru Joyce, sophomore guard—He had one of the outstanding individual performances in state championship history last year, shooting 7-of-7 from 3-point range for 21 points. His dad, Dru Sr., is an assistant coach, and his younger brother, Cameron, is a ballboy. Joyce stands 5-foot-5 and hopes to become a college basketball coach. And, believe it or not, this mild-mannered kid said that he's learned to control his anger since being at St. V-M. Go figure.
- Carlos Mays, sophomore forward—His hobby is drawing and he wants to be an archaeologist.
- Willie McGee, sophomore guard—He carries a 3.1 GPA and wants to coach or own his own business. He likes R&B, and has learned to depend on others while on the team.
- William McWain, senior guard—Known as "P-Dub," he wants to study psychology in college. For now, he's the team comedian. His trademark routine is his impression of Coach Keith Dambrot.

- Chad Mraz, junior guard—He has been out with a knee injury all season but his house is the gathering place and he is the cheerleader on the bench. While recuperating, Mraz has perfected the art of growing an Afro. He's an exceptional student, carrying a 3.6 GPA.
- Aly Samabaly, senior guard—His sister, who is 31 and was his guardian, sent him to the United States to live. He carries a 3.1 GPA and wants to pursue a career in international business. He speaks eight languages.
- Preston Sims, freshman forward—He wants to own his business and is looking for a girl with a "nice personality."
- John Taylor, senior guard—If Richie Cunningham (*Happy Days*) played basketball in real life, he'd be Taylor. He's the All-American kid who wears a size 13.
- Romeo Travis, sophomore center/forward—He has an interesting hobby: sleeping. When he's awake, he likes to study business management. His favorite food is chicken "with a lot of hot sauce on it."
- Brandon Weems, freshman guard—He's listed at 5-7, and if that's true, then Joyce is 6-5. Weems is the ultimate student-athlete. He carries a 4.1 GPA and collects shoes. His funniest experience as a player? "P-Dubs' impression of Coach."

AUTHOR'S INSPIRATION

One day while I was at St. Vincent-St. Mary for a practice, Ann Garber came up with an idea that she thought would be interesting for a story. I went to her office where she had questionnaires that were filled out by LeBron and the rest of the team. The questions were simple, like "What is your favorite food? What is your favorite movie" etc.

I thought it would be fun to take out a few items from each player and write a sentence about their interests so that the general public could get a little closer to these guys.

Oak Hill Wins War: James Shines, Rest of Irish Fall Short 72-66

St. Vincent-St. Mary's LeBron James and Oak Hill Academy's Carmelo Anthony turned Sovereign Bank Arena into their own one-on-one playground battle during yesterday's Prime Time Shootout.

The two players, both projected to be future first-round NBA picks, had a stretch during the third quarter where they tried to one-up each other.

Anthony, a 6-foot-7 senior guard/forward, came down and put a move on James, which drew oohs and aahs from the crowd of more than 6,000. Anthony finished with 34 points.

James, a 6-7 junior guard/forward, isn't one to be upstaged. So on the next play, James brought the ball up court, knifed his way through the lane and slammed the ball through the net.

It went back and forth like that for three or four possessions.

James finished with a game-high 36 points, but it was Anthony and the Warriors who came out on top as Oak Hill defeated St. V-M 72-66 in a battle of two of the nation's elite teams.

Oak Hill (26-1) is ranked No. 4 in the country. St. V-M (15-2) is ranked No. 5.

When play was stopped with just three seconds left in the game because of a foul, the crowd rose to its feet and applauded.

"It was a great game and I think the fans were applauding all the players, not just Anthony and LeBron," Oak Hill coach Steve Smith said. "But those two are exceptional players."

Take James and Anthony out of the equation, and the difference in this game came down to the rest of the players.

Oak Hill's starters minus Anthony combined for 38 points, with 6-10 senior forward Sani Ibrahim scoring 16. St. V-M's starters minus James scored 28.

"Not to take anything away from (St. V-M's) players but I think our supporting cast did a better job of helping Carmelo than their supporting cast did of helping LeBron," Smith said.

Oak Hill was able to expose a few of St. V-M's weaknesses. First, the Warriors were bigger and stronger all-around, and the Irish couldn't get into a flow. The Irish trailed 12-2 with 4:36 left in the opening quarter.

"We've had a history of having guys get more than they should in the paint and we let them get the ball in the paint in transition," Coach Dru Joyce II said about Oak Hill's fast start. "They were too big for us to let that happen. They were just tough to defend."

The Irish trailed by as many as 12 points in the first half but cut the lead to eight (34-28) at halftime. "We didn't start to get into a rhythm until the second quarter and that was too late," Dru Joyce III said.

The Warriors pushed the lead to 50-35 on a dunk by Anthony late in the third quarter, and that's when it looked like the Irish were done. But St. V-M battled back and cut the lead to 54-51 on a three-point play by James with 5:46 left.

James then hit a 3-pointer with 37 seconds left to cut Oak Hill's lead to 69-64. That prompted Smith to call for a timeout.

When the Warriors tried inbounding the ball after the timeout at St. V-M's end of the court, Sekou Lewis (nine points) stole the ball in the corner and passed it to Joyce III, whose wide-open 3-point attempt went in and out.

Joyce III's shot would've cut the lead to 69-67. Lewis, however, crashed the board and his tip rolled in and out of the rim and was rebounded by Ibrahim, who was fouled and made both free throws with 27.2 seconds left for a 71-64 lead.

Romeo Travis (eight points) scored St. V-M's final basket with 17 seconds left, and Oak Hill added a free throw for the final points.

"This is the only time all season that we were considered underdogs," Coach Joyce II said. "We weren't expected to win but our guys felt they could win. We have a lot of things to work on and we'll learn from this game and get better because our main goal all year has been to win a state championship."

AUTHOR'S INSPIRATION

This was yet another milestone game for LeBron and St. Vincent-St. Mary because it was another rematch against national-power Oak Hill, which featured future NBA All-Star Carmelo Anthony. The hype leading up to this game was incredible and the people in Trenton, N.J. and the surrounding area was excited about the matchup between the top two high school players in the country.

While covering the event, before, during and after, I was amazed yet again by the energy and excitement LeBron and the Irish always seemed to produce whenever they played—whether it was at home or on the road. St. Vincent-St. Mary lost this one, but it was one of a few losses LeBron ever experienced in his high school career.

Cover Boy Is All Smiles: St. Vincent-St. Mary's James Thrilled to Grace Sports Illustrated *Front*

Another day, another article on St. Vincent-St. Mary basketball star LeBron James. Only this time, the article is in this week's issue of *Sports Illustrated* and James is on the cover with the words "The Chosen One" describing the phenom. "Just think about the company LeBron is in," said assistant football coach Joe Hoffman, who was at a news conference yesterday at the school as James talked about being featured in the article. "Jesse Owens, Mickey Mantle, Willie Mays, Michael Jordan, Muhammad Ali and LeBron. It's just mind-boggling. I have goose bumps just thinking about it."

Imagine that. A 41-year-old man rolling up his sleeve and showing the goose bumps all over his arms as he talks about a 17-year-old kid.

But we all know James isn't your ordinary 17-year-old junior playing basketball. James is considered the best high school player in the country. Now, the center of the high school basketball universe is Akron. "I love this school and there isn't anywhere else I'd want to play and I'm glad the article is bringing exposure to the team, the school and Akron," James said. But LeBron, don't you just love seeing yourself on the cover of one of the most popular sports magazines in the world?

"Yeah, I think I look really good," James said with a big smile. "I knew they were thinking about putting me on the cover but with the Super Bowl and the Winter Olympics, I wasn't sure. I'm happy they put me on the cover."

And get this—James doesn't even have a subscription to *Sports Illustrated*. *SI* writer Grant Wahl followed James around for three days last week and James spent an entire day posing for a *Sports Illustrated* photographer for the cover shot.

"We started shooting here at the school around 8 o'clock in the morning on a Saturday and I was really tired," James said. "They took about 100 pictures and it took me awhile to get into it. They had to go out and get me orange juice and fruit to wake me up and get me some energy. But it was fun."

If you haven't seen the cover, James is posing with a gold basketball in his hand and his face covered with what appears to be sweat. "That wasn't really sweat," he revealed. "They put water on my face to make it look like I was sweating." The article has an interesting comment from former Phoenix Suns coach and former NBA player Danny Ainge. He said there are only a few players in the NBA that he wouldn't trade to get James right now. James is considered to be the No. 1 pick in the draft if he Acame out this year, which James said isn't going to happen.

"I want to win a state championship this year and come back next year and do it again," he said. No longer is James just a local story. With *SI* magazines hitting some newsstands yesterday and in subscribers' mail boxes today, James is an international story. But what makes James so special is the way he keeps his "star status" in perspective. It would be very easy for such a gifted athlete such as James to be overwhelmed by the national attention.

Not James. Loyalty is one of his strongest qualities. And he's one of the most charismatic teenagers you'll ever meet. He always remembers those who have been by his side. "My friends have been with me since the fourth grade," James said, speaking of teammates Dru Joyce III, Willie McGee and Sian Cotton. "They are all like brothers to me." And I love all my teammates like family. There isn't anything I wouldn't do for them."

AUTHOR'S INSPIRATION

When a grown man told me that he got goosebumps after seeing LeBron James on the cover of *Sports Illustrated*, that's when I knew things may be out of control. Actually, the *SI* cover and all the exposure that came after the magazine hit the stand is exactly what prompted me to write a book about LeBron, entitled, *LeBron James: The Rise of A Star*.

The whole atmosphere surrounding LeBron and his teammates at St. V-M was so unbelievable, I just knew I had to chronicle what was going on somehow. I didn't know how, I just knew someone needed to keep record of everything that was going on.

A few months later, I went to LeBron's mother, Gloria, about writing a book about her son. She responded, "Give me some time and let me talk to 'Bron." Not long after that, Gloria and LeBron gave me the OK to write the book.

James Is Handling Flood Well: Irish Junior Superstar Remains as Close to a Normal High School Kid as Possible

I receive emails and telephone calls on a regular basis from people complaining about media coverage of LeBron James. "I'm tired of reading the LeBron *Beacon Journal*," one caller said. The only thing I can say is, "Get used to it." We're talking about a player who some NBA experts say would be the first pick in the NBA Draft if he came out this year.

We're talking about a kid who next Sunday will be named first-team All-American by *Parade Magazine* for the second consecutive year. Also, he is *Parade*'s national Player of the Year selection. He has won Ohio's Mr. Basketball award for the second consecutive year. When he won it last year, he was the first sophomore in history to do so.

As the Irish (23-3) prepare to face Cincinnati St. Bernard Roger Bacon (24-3) today in the Division II state championship game in Columbus, they are in line to become just the third team in Ohio history to win three consecutive state titles.

So, James and the Irish will continue to be the hot topic until his high school career is over. You have to credit James, however, for being mature enough to handle all the media attention, which includes being featured on the cover of *Sports Illustrated*. There are critics who say he showboats after dunks and sometimes is arrogant and doesn't show class on the court. Sure, James went overboard against Hoban when he took a lap around the court at Rhodes Arena after a spectacular dunk and a timeout by Hoban.

But what about the fans who yell "overrated" when James doesn't score as many points as fans think that he should score. Or the ones who chant "high school dropout," which insinuates that James will leave high school after this year to enter the draft. James hears those comments.

How does he handle it? "It doesn't bother me because I'm just doing what I love to do," James said.

This is still a 17-year-old high school junior who likes to hang out with his teammates. He likes to attend school functions and support the other sports programs. For instance, James traveled with other schoolmates to Columbus to watch St. V-M participate in the state wrestling tournament last month. James also attended several girls soccer games and is a regular at freshman boys basketball games.

"LeBron is a hoot at those games," said Renata Ochsenhirt, whose son Mark is a freshman on the team. "And (teammate) Romeo (Travis) is always mooching your candy." James and several teammates showed up at the school's production of Annie. That was for extra credit classwork, though.

And one day during lunch a few months ago, James brought in three bags filled with extra athletic gear that he has received during the past few years and gave it all away. He made a game out of it by having students answer questions such as "What's my mom's name?" or, "How tall is Dru (Joyce III)?" James gave away three new pairs of tennis shoes, basketball shorts, gym bags, headbands and hats that hadn't been worn.

The bottom line is that James is trying to do the right thing, even when critics think he isn't.

AUTHOR'S INSPIRATION

During LeBron's high school career and long after that, critics continued to judge LeBron on so many levels and until he retires, the critics will always be out there.

But I often times wondered why so many people felt the need to criticize him during his high school years. He was blessed with amazing skills. Sure, he got a big head at times. The reality is I've seen student-athletes with WAY less talent than LeBron in high school who had WAY bigger egos than LeBron did. And I'm sure you've come across those people.

LeBron was no different than any other high school superstar athlete. He had moments of arrogance. He had moments of sincerity. He could be crude in the hallways or in public, then again, he was likeable and funny. The only difference, and the BIG difference, is that he was worth millions of dollars while he was still in high school.

Think about this. LeBron signed a $90 million endorsement deal with Nike in April of his senior year, which meant he was still enrolled at St. V-M and going to classes. Imagine a classmate walking up to LeBron while the two are in the lunch line the next day.

"Hey LeBron, did you do anything fun last night?"

"Not really. Let me think. I went to practice, went home, ate dinner . . . no, nothing I can think of. Oh wait . . . I did sign a $90 million contract with Nike. My bad."

Then, LeBron gets to the cashier, who says, "That'll be $4.50."

Three Was Just Not to Be: Fighting Irish Lose in Bid for Third Consecutive State Title

There was no three-peat for the St. Vincent-St. Mary boys basketball team this year. Cincinnati St. Bernard Roger Bacon made sure of that.

St. V-M went into the Division II state championship game yesterday at Ohio State's Value City Arena trying to become just the third team in Ohio high school history to win three consecutive titles. Roger Bacon, however, went into the game with a score to settle after St. V-M had defeated the Spartans 79-70 in December at the M.A.C. Center.

"We all remembered that feeling after that loss," said 6-foot-8 junior center Monty St. Clair. "I had never seen our locker room the way it was. We made a promise that we would see (St. V-M) in the state finals."

That wish came true, and Roger Bacon took care of business, defeating the Irish 71-63 before a record crowd of 18,375.

"We have nothing to feel bad about," Irish coach Dru Joyce II said. "We had a great season, and I'm not going to let one game dictate who we are as a team.

"Of course we wanted to win, but Roger Bacon wanted it a little bit more and they outplayed us."

The Spartans balanced attack had four players in double figures, with Josh Hausfeld leading the way with 23 points, plus an effective defense. They also dominated the boards, outrebounding the Irish 32-18. "They are fundamentally sound so they don't make a lot of mistakes, that's why they are an outstanding team," Joyce II said. "They were big inside, and they hurt us."

St. Clair finished with 15 points for Roger Bacon, followed by Beckham Wyrick (14 points) and Frank Phillips (13).

LeBron James led St. V-M (23-4) with 32 points, and his total of three rebounds illustrated how Roger Bacon controlled the boards. Romeo Travis, the Irish's other low post threat, fouled out late in the fourth quarter, finishing with 19 points and nine rebounds.

James tried to look at the positives. "Coming into the season, people didn't think we would make it this far with a new head coach," he said. "We had three losses, but they were against good teams. I think we had one of the toughest schedules in the country.

"I'm an All-American with a lot of good role players," James said. "Oak Hill (Va.) has five All-Americans on that team and Amityville (N.Y.) has two. But we still played with these teams and it says a lot about the kind of teammates I have."

During the regular season, St. V-M lost to Oak Hill 72-66 and Amityville 84-83.

Before the game, tickets were being scalped for as much as $150. Inside the arena, fans probably figured the game would go down to the wire after watching Roger Bacon stay with St. V-M for the first two quarters.

The Spartans trailed 17-15 after the first quarter but led 31-30 at halftime. During the first half, St. V-M struggled on defense, allowing several easy layups.

"Defensively, we had some breakdowns and it was a matter of us not fighting through screens," Joyce said.

Then Roger Bacon built a lead of 11 points (48-37) with 3:26 left in the third quarter.

But St. V-M rallied late in the quarter, and the Irish cut the lead to 51-46 heading into the final period. James hit a 3-pointer just a few steps beyond mid-court as the third-quarter horn sounded.

The Spartans built another lead of nine points at 57-48 with 5:45 remaining in the game when St. V-M made a run.

The Irish cut the lead to 59-56 with 2:58 to play on a dunk by James. Then St. V-M pulled within two points at 60-58, when James scored and was fouled inside with 2:17 left.

James missed the free throw, but the Irish got the ball back on a Roger Bacon turnover and had the chance to tie the score or take the lead. But they couldn't capitalize.

The Irish came within two points again (65-63) after James completed a three-point play, but the Spartans held off St. V-M at the free-throw line in the final 30 seconds.

One of the free throws came after a technical foul on Joyces son, Irish junior point guard Dru Joyce III. He was called for a "T" with eight seconds remaining and Roger Bacon leading 66-63. He threw the ball at the rim after a foul was called on the Irish.

After the game, Joyce III started to walk into the locker room, but Coach Joyce ran toward the locker area and brought his son back into the arena. "That was frustration," Joyce II said. "He's believing right now that the technical cost us the game, but it didn't. Our guys just needed to understand that we were going to show class and applaud Roger Bacon and wish them well because they were the better team.

"Right now, the loss hurts but tomorrow it's not going to hurt as much and the day after that, it will hurt even less. As time goes by, they'll be thankful for this opportunity. It just didn't work out in our favor this time."

For Roger Bacon (25-3), it was the Spartans' first state title since 1982.

AUTHOR'S INSPIRATION

In my personal opinion, this loss was probably the biggest motivating factor in LeBron becoming the intense and focused player he went on to become in the NBA, and let me explain.

After the final horn sounded and the Irish were dealt the disappointing upset, several of LeBron's teammates were on the court crying. But not LeBron. He went down the court and shook the hands of each and every player on Roger Bacon's team, congratulated them and showed the utmost sportsmanship and respect. Once we got into the postgame interview room and started the press conference, LeBron's teammates were still upset. But LeBron was very composed and it really surprised me. Actually, it shocked me, because for as competitive as LeBron was, I just knew he would have taken this loss the hardest.

But it was the opposite. I asked LeBron what was next for him and he said that he was going to take a few weeks off to rest, then he was going to get back into the weight room and the gym and was going to work harder than he ever had in his life so that "I never, ever have to experience this feeling again."

That game was in late March. About four months later, I ran into LeBron at a local gas station and I couldn't believe my eyes. He had grown a few inches but what was obvious was that he had transformed himself from a tall, wiry, basketball player to a muscular, absolutly chiseled man-child. I was almost speechless as I looked at how ripped he was.

And all I could do was think back to that day in Columbus, during the press conference, when LeBron made that statement about him coming back for his senior year stronger, hungrier and coming back with a vengeance. Coming back with a purpose.

He did.

Vitale Gets Chance to See James Play: He'll Be Part of ESPN2 Team for Oak Hill Game

When it was announced that St. Vincent-St. Mary's Dec. 12 basketball game against Oak Hill (Va.) Academy at the Cleveland State Convocation Center would be televised nationally by ESPN2, Irish star LeBron James had an idea. James thought it would be great if veteran announcer Dick Vitale would call the game.

James got his wish. One announcer will be Vitale, and the other could be former UCLA and NBA great Bill Walton. The game, expected to be a sellout, is now being called "The High School Classic." The prime seating tickets, priced at $35, have already sold out.

While it might be a high school game, Vitale said he is excited about seeing James play in person for the first time. "If this kid is half as good as people say, then we're in for a big treat," said Vitale.

Vitale said he has been impressed with the way James is handling the publicity and attention as one of the most talked-about high school players. "Usually with young players, you hear a lot of negative, but I haven't heard anything negative about the kid," Vitale said.

James has also caught the attention of other national broadcasters. Clark Kellogg, a former Cleveland St. Joseph's player who later went on to star at Ohio State and the NBA, said Vitale is the perfect choice to broadcast the high school game.

"Dick has fun with it because he enjoys what he does, he's great at what he does and he's passionate about the kids," said Kellogg, who is a basketball analyst for CBS and lives in the Columbus suburb of Westerville.

However, another CBS analyst, Billy Packer, says the James phenomenon has a down side. "I am very much against the promotion of high school athletes as if they have accomplished something beyond high school athleticism," he said. "If I were assigned to do that game, I wouldn't broadcast it.

"I feel the hyping of kids before they are ready to be productive at the next level is part of what has destroyed the fabric of sports in America and I think this is more of the same," Packer said.

Kellogg, who scored 51 points in the 1979 state championship game against Columbus East, said he can relate, somewhat, to the media hype surrounding James.

When Kellogg was a senior in high school, he was considered one of the top players in the country.

"The hype machine is ten-fold what it was, say, 20 or 30 years ago," Kellogg said. "I got a decent amount of notoriety but when I played (in high school), there was no *USA Today* and ESPN was in its infancy. But with the Internet and all of the 24-hour news sources now, the gifted players will get their notoriety. That's the highway we're on."

Kellogg led Ohio State in scoring and rebounding in his sophomore and junior seasons, earning All-Big Ten honors, and entered the NBA draft after his junior season as the Indiana Pacers' No. 1 pick.

Kellogg said he has never seen James play in person, but his father did last year at the Canton Fieldhouse when the Irish played Orange.

"My dad doesn't give out praise lightly but he told me how good LeBron is and I was sold on it," Kellogg said.

Asked about all the attention devoted to a high school player, Kellogg said: "I have mixed emotions. In some ways it's good to expose all sides of athletics, but in some ways it's a detriment because it glamorizes the results instead of the process."

AUTHOR'S INSPIRATION

It was interesting to interview members of the national media, like Dick Vitale, Clark Kellogg and Billy Packer to get their perspectives on a player like LeBron. I never felt like I needed to be LeBron's publicist, but I would always chuckle (to myself) when I would hear people like Billy Packer criticize the notoriety LeBron was getting because he hadn't proved anything beyond high school. I respect Billy Packer and respect his opinion, but I knew LeBron was going to be a great pro in the NBA (and I stated that on national television shows before he ever played his first game) because of what I saw in him for four years. The ability, intellect and maturity he possessed at the high school level was something that I had never seen in my lifetime. And I think it's something I won't see again in my lifetime.

OHSAA Inquiry Ongoing: Muscaro Says Focus on Purchase of Hummer

The Ohio High School Athletic Association's inquiry into basketball star LeBron James' Hummer vehicle is continuing.

"All I can say is that the investigation is still ongoing," Commissioner Clair Muscaro said Tuesday.

Asked if the investigation was heading in a different direction, Muscaro said: "No. We're just concentrating on the vehicle."

Last week, the OHSAA expressed concerns about the Hummer sports utility vehicle purchased by Gloria James, mother of St. Vincent-St. Mary star basketball player LeBron James, who is projected by some experts to be the No. 1 pick in the NBA Draft in June.

OHSAA bylaw 4-10-1 (c) states that an athlete forfeits amateur status by "capitalizing on athletic fame by receiving money or gifts."

Muscaro wanted documentation from Gloria James proving that she is the one who obtained the loan to purchase the 2003 Hummer H2, which is valued at more than $50,000.

A family source who asked not to be identified said last week that Gloria James did receive a loan from a bank in Columbus and that the information was sent to the OHSAA from the bank.

Officials at the OHSAA said the school isn't being investigated.

St. V-M currently is 12-0 and ranked the No. 1 team in the country, according to the latest *USA Today* poll. The Irish defeated R.J. Reynolds 85-56 Monday at the Greensboro (N.C.) Coliseum, in front of a crowd of more than 15,000, which was the largest crowd to see a high school game in North Carolina history.

AUTHOR'S INSPIRATION

This was the first of two incidents surrounding LeBron that gathered national attention. How could a kid, who's mother live in subsidized housing, afford to buy a $53,000 Hummer? The answer was simple. Gloria got a loan.

Jonathan Lampley epitomized the term "student-athlete" with his performance on the court and in the classroom. Courtesy of VSN Photography.

Adam Hamad takes a moment with his mother, Sandy, during Senior Night at an Archbishop Hoban Knights football game. Courtesy of Chris Hamad.

Mylan Murphy didn't let a knee injury stop his dream of playing college basketball and starting a non-profit Christian organization called Strive4. Courtesy of the Murphy Family.

As members of the McDonald's All-American boys team look on, Candace Parker makes the winning slam dunk. Courtesy of McDonald's Corporation.

Eddie Ponder and his daughter, Nicole, during halftime of a football game. Courtesy of Courtney Ponder.

Akron Ellet assistant football coach Gary Yost and his wife, Tobi. Courtesy of the Yost Family.

Indians infielder Jhonny Peralta and Amy Tausch. Courtesy of Betsy Tausch.

Marc Leffler was thrust into the starting quarterback role in the first game as a freshman at Akron Ellet High School and performed admirably. Courtesy of the Leffler Family.

Former wrestling coach Ralph Paonessa is with his daughter, Angela, his grandson Nick and wife Nanci after his 2002 induction into the Archbishop Hoban High School Hall of Fame. Courtesy of the Paonessa Family.

The Brennan family frequently traveled to the Dominican Republic to share their love for baseball and their Christian faith. Courtesy of the Brennan Family.

Jordan Poth possessed all the qualities needed to be a star quarterback. Courtesy of Kimberly Jeter, Mogadore Youth Football.

Carla L. (Chapman) Sibley gives instruction to her boys varsity basketball team at Akron Garfield High School. Courtesy of Jeff Sibley.

Now, I couldn't have walked into a loan institution and asked for a $53,000 loan for a Hummer. I would've been laughed out of the building. But not Gloria. She got the loan and it's easy to see how. The loan institution knew who they were dealing with and they knew they would be getting their money back. Plain and simple.

52-Pickup For LeBron: James Ties Opponent. St. V-M Defeats Westchester 78-52

The last time St. Vincent-St. Mary senior LeBron James played at the Sovereign Bank Arena, it was a performance to remember.

This time, it was a performance for the record books.

James scored a school-record 52 points Saturday as top-ranked St. V-M defeated Los Angeles Westchester 78-52 in the Prime Time Shoot Out in front of a sellout crowd of 8,500.

The Irish played Oak Hill Academy in last season's Prime Time Shoot Out, and it was exactly that—a shootout.

James finished with a game-high 36 points, outdueling Carmelo Anthony, who had 34. But Anthony, now a freshman starter at Syracuse, got the last laugh as Oak Hill defeated St. V-M by six points.

This time, James wasn't leaving the arena with a loss.

James' previous high was 50 against Mentor last month at Rhodes Arena.

"It felt good," said James, as close to 100 media members attended the postgame news conference. "Maybe it was the crowd that got me going, I don't know. I just like playing here. Last year, we had a great game with Carmelo Anthony. We just have to keep handling business."

James also hinted that he was able to respond after facing adversity. For instance, after the Hummer investigation, James pumped in 50 against Mentor. Saturday night was James' first game back since being ruled ineligible by the Ohio High School Athletic Association last Friday for accepting gifts.

A Summit County judge granted a temporary restraining order Wednesday that allowed him to play. "Maybe if something else comes up, I'll score 52 again," he joked. "No, when you make mistakes, you have to learn from them and move on."

It was just one of those games for James. His outside shot was falling, and when he's feeling good on the perimeter, he's tough to defend.

"I feel like when my jumper is on, I'm unstoppable," James said. "Once you get the jumper going, it opens up the inside game and it opens up your whole arsenal."

Right from the start, it was apparent that it was going to be a good night for James. He scored 18 of St. V-M's 20 first-quarter points as the Irish (15-1) took a 20-14 lead. St. V-M trailed 6-4 but James scored 10 consecutive points as the Irish took the lead.

James continued his offensive barrage in the second quarter with 13 points, and St. V-M used a 16-4 run to end the half with a 41-24 lead. James had 31 in the first two quarters.

"I figured he could have one of those nights and he did," said Westchester coach Ed Azzam, whose team is 22-3 and ranked No. 7 by *USA Today*. "He was knocking down those outside shots. He had a great night."

The Comets have two outstanding players in Trevor Azira and Scott Cutley. Azira is a UCLA recruit, and Cutley is headed to Kent State. Azira finished with 12 points, while Cutley scored just six. The Irish didn't have any other players score in double figures.

When St. V-M needed shots from the outside, James, Corey Jones and Dru Joyce III delivered. When the Irish needed strong moves inside, it was James and Romeo Travis getting it done. When they needed to play strong defense to prevent Westchester from getting back into the game, they did that too. "We're all about playing defense," James said. "When you work hard on defense, you'll always give yourself a chance to win."

The crowd witnessed a splendid performance by James. But one fan probably will never forget this game.

James had just stolen the ball and finished the play with a dunk, which prompted Azzam to call a timeout. The dunk brought the crowd to its feet. As James was about to walk off the court, Jovan Marino, a ballboy, ran onto the court and jumped right into James' arms, and the star basketball player gave the little guy a hug. "I just jumped up in his arms like that was my dad," said Marino, who also got James' autograph after the game. "It was like he gave me a present."

AUTHOR'S INSPIRATION

This was LeBron's first game back after being reinstated following "Jerseygate." One thing I can truly say is that whenever LeBron was faced with some kind of adversity, he ALWAYS rose to the occasion, like he did in this case.

Called for Traveling: Planes, Fame and Automobiles Make St. V-M's Season 15,000 Miles Long

When the season is over, St. Vincent-St. Mary basketball team will have logged more than 15,000 miles. The Irish played games in Pittsburgh, Philadelphia, Los Angeles, Greensboro, N.C., Trenton, N.J., Dayton and Columbus. The players walked through airports and boarded planes and turned the heads of other passengers.

"They probably think we're a college team," LeBron James said. "It's pretty fun going all over the place and having fans come out to see us. We know we're giving them entertainment, but we're just doing what we love to do."

Carolyn Joyce, wife of Coach Dru Joyce II, and Debra Cotton, wife of assistant coach Lee Cotton, were the informal "team moms" and grew accustomed to the travel.

"It is the same as it was when all the boys were playing AAU together," Carolyn Joyce said. "We're used to doing this and the kids are like our sons."

Debra Cotton noticed a difference from the AAU days. "Now, when you get off the plane, cameras are right there and it can be hectic at times," she said. "But it's still a lot of fun and it's still exciting. It's an extension of what we've been doing the past eight or nine years."

The players had some time to kill when they weren't practicing basketball or doing homework. What did they do?

"We do a lot of roastin'," James said.

Roastin' is like crackin'. Crackin' is like playin' the dozens.

Playin' the dozens is like this:

"Your mother is so fat, when she sits around the house, she really sits around the house."

That's what high school kids do, at least the St. V-M team, when they are killing time in their hotel rooms.

Roastin' is just one way the team comes together.

"We're very close as a team," said senior forward Sian Cotton, who will play football next season at Ohio State. "When we're on the road, all we have is each other. "We crack up roastin' each other, but it's all in fun."

Video games are popular, too—when Coach Joyce allows them. "There is work that needs to be done when we're on the road and we need to be focused, but they are teenagers and they should have fun," he said. "They get in their rooms and laugh and joke and that's building camaraderie."

James claims he's the reigning PlayStation champ in NBA Live 2003, Madden 2003 and College Basketball 2003.

"Ask any of them; they'll tell you who's the best," James said.

Freshman Brian Glasper II had another story.

"LeBron will tell you he's the champ, but (sophomore) Marcus Allen beat him in NBA 2003," Glasper said.

Freshman Matt Ochsenhirt took it one step further. "I think Marcus beat LeBron twice," he said.

Glasper, whose nickname is "LB," and Ochsenhirt don't see a lot of playing time, but they realize how lucky they are to have the opportunity to play on such a talented team and to have the chance to travel.

"This has been a great experience for me, especially being only a freshman," said Glasper, who was the leading receiver on the varsity football team.

That goes for his father and namesake. "Traveling with the team and meeting new people, I really think it has broken the racial barrier," the elder Glasper said. "We all get along because we're all here supporting the kids.

"It's more than just basketball and these kids have brought the adults together—adults from all walks of life. We've all become a family."

It has been a great first varsity season for Ochsenhirt. "I'll always remember this," he said. "The travel can get tiring sometimes because we're not allowed to miss school, but it's worth it. And even though I don't get to play a lot, I know some of the younger guys are making the older guys better in practice. We know our time will come."

Parents Nancy and Tim Ochsenhirt have followed the team on the road all year. "These kids are traveling all over the place and they've had to grow up really fast, which is unfortunate because you really want them to have fun and understand how special this is," Nancy Ochsenhirt said. "I know I'll never be able to explain what this year has been like. There aren't words to describe it."

Freshmen Patrick Nygaard and Blaise Meeker and sophomore Jazmin Garrett also are players who see action only at the end of games. It doesn't matter to them or their parents. "When we get to the airport, everybody knows LeBron and all their heads turn," Nygaard said. "It's pretty sweet knowing you're part of all that." Nygaard got a chance to play at the Palestra but didn't get in at the famed Pauley Pavilion. His dad, Kurt, didn't care.

"Just to be a freshman and get the chance to even warm up at Pauley Pavilion, where UCLA won so many national championships, is not only a treat for Patrick, but it's a treat for Dad as well. It doesn't get any better than that," he said.

Traveling all over the country isn't new to James, but he likes seeing the younger players enjoying the experience. "You can see it in their faces that they are having fun, and that's what it should be all about," James said.

Garrett said parts of the traveling have been overwhelming. "Sometimes it's weird traveling everywhere because you'll see somebody in a hotel that you've never met before and they talk to you like they've known you forever," he said. "It's strange. But it's cool being with my teammates because we're pretty much around each other more than we are our own family.

"It's also a great feeling being in your room and watching ESPN and seeing our team on national television. Even though the spotlight is on LeBron, every once in a while, one of us will walk by the screen and we'll get on TV."

Garrett's mother, Dawnisha, and her daughter, who has the same name, rarely miss a game. "I go wherever my son goes," she said.

Jazmin Garrett said he can always spot his mother and sister. "No matter how loud it is in a the gym, I can always hear my mother and sister. I love having them there, especially on the road," he said.

As the Irish (17-1) play the last of their regular-season road games today against Kettering Alter in Dayton, they can look back on having played at Philadelphia's legendary Palestra before a sellout crowd of more than 8,500. The contest at UCLA's Pauley Pavilion against Mater Dei of Santa Ana, Calif., drew 15,000-plus, as did the game at the Greensboro Coliseum against R.J. Reynolds. That crowd was the largest in North Carolina high school history.

Christine and Tom Marks jokingly concede that it might take five years to pay off their Visa bill, but they said traveling with the team has been worth every penny. The Marks' son, Tim, is a junior who came off the bench early in the year, but a knee injury in the second game ended his season.

Still, Marks travels with the team and offers support at the end of the bench, and his parents have made every trip. "We talked about it before the season and our goal was to go where the team played, no matter what it took," Christine Marks said. "Getting off work is an issue, and of course the financial aspect of traveling, but we looked at it as a once-in-a-lifetime chance for us and our son."

AUTHOR'S INSPIRATION

Most high school teams take the customary yellow school bus to their games. Not St. Vincent-St. Mary. The Irish played all over the country during LeBron's senior year. On several occasions, the team would take a chartered bus to the Akron-Canton regional airport where they would then fly to different parts of the country for their games.

The whole LeBron four-year experience was like a dream and I'm sure we'll never see anything like it ever again.

LeBron Emotional at Movie Premiere, Documentary Is a Hit at Toronto Film Festival

Kristopher Belman, an Akron native turned Hollywood filmmaker, couldn't have come up with a more appropriate title for his extremely entertaining and revealing documentary *More Than a Game*, which was a huge hit during its premiere Saturday at the Toronto International Film Festival.

The movie features the story of Cavaliers superstar LeBron James and his "Fab Five" friends—Dru Joyce III, Sian Cotton, Willie McGee and Romeo Travis—who won a national basketball championship at St. Vincent-St. Mary High School during their senior season.

Using never-before-seen home videos, pictures and exclusive interviews from LeBron, his longtime friends, and a host of family members, Belman delivered a poignant film that opens up the personal life of not only LeBron, but also the lives of every person who has meant something to LeBron, including his mother, Gloria.

You don't need to be a movie critic to know this film will be a success. Belman did a fantastic job extracting interesting and personal stories from the cast. To do that, he needed to establish love, friendship, loyalty and trust for—and from—his cast members when he met them in 2003. He did so when he started this project as a senior at Loyola Marymount University in Los Angeles, a school nationally known for its film program.

I had to fight back a few tears as I sat in the theater watching the film, and I'm sure there were many others in the sold-out crowd of 1,200 at Ryerson Theatre who felt the same way.

The film, for which LeBron is the executive producer, is more than a bunch of kids playing basketball, winning games and being cocky. It's more than a filmmaker trying to make a quick buck by capitalizing on LeBron's fame. It's LeBron's personal story.

How emotional was the film for LeBron? After the screening, which earned a roaring standing ovation from the audience, the principal cast members (the Fab Five, along with St. V-M coach Dru Joyce II) left their seats in the front of the theater and went onstage for a question-and-answer session with the audience.

The Q&A never happened, however, because LeBron and his friends spent the 20-plus minutes expressing their feelings openly and publicly to the audience.

LeBron thanked the audience for coming. He thanked Belman, whom the players continue to call "Cameraman" instead of Kris, for doing such a wonderful job. He thanked Joyce and Travis for flying nine hours from Germany, where they are playing basketball professionally, to attend the event.

Belman effectively captured the essence of the film, which was friendship, loyalty, trust and love, LeBron said. Then, LeBron, a 6-foot-8, 260-pound man who has carried an NBA franchise on his back since his rookie season at age 18, stopped talking and started to get choked up.

He cried onstage. For the first time, the public witnessed a deeply emotional moment for LeBron. "This is the first time I've cried—in basketball or anything—since we lost that national championship game in eighth grade," LeBron said, referring to an AAU game in Orlando.

He wasn't the only one who cried. When Travis took the microphone, he commented about the film and before he could get through his thank-yous, he paused so he wouldn't break down.

But he did. Same with coach Joyce.

There are at least four moments in the movie that will have you fighting the urge to just say, "Ahh."

An insider associated with the movie said Belman had a tough time selling his idea to Hollywood. "Typically, people in Hollywood automatically say, 'No, no, no,' before even hearing or seeing an idea," the individual said. Belman never gave up and eventually met Harvey Mason Jr., the film's producer. Before backing Belman, Mason made a name for himself in the music industry and is well respected on the West Coast.

Mason and Damon Thomas, the production team that is The Underdogs, were responsible for the soundtrack of the award-winning 2006 film *Dreamgirls*. Mason gave Belman the backing he needed three years ago because they trusted each other, and Mason believed in Belman, just as James and his friends believed in Belman.

After the audience left the theater, all I could do was wonder what others will think of the movie once it's bought and distributed in U.S. theaters. Will they be critical and cynical when it comes to LeBron and his rags-to-riches story? Will they continue, as some do, to think of LeBron as a pompous, arrogant, self-glorifying professional athlete?

Or will they, like the audience at Saturday's showing at the Ryerson Theatre, sit back with an open mind, watch the film and be entertained and moved like my wife and I and hundreds of other spectators? My guess is that most audiences thoroughly will enjoy this film because it is *More Than a Game,* as Belman put it.

AUTHOR'S INSPIRATION:

My good friend Kris Belman and I go back to LeBron's days in high school. I was working on my book *LeBron James: The Rise Of A Star* and Kris, an Akron native who was a film student at Loyola Marymount University in Los Angeles who was working on his senior project. He was working on a 12- to 15-minute documentary on not just LeBron, but the entire St. Vincent-St. Mary team LeBron's senior year. There were many nights when Kris would come over and enjoy a nice, homemade spaghetti dinner prepared by my wife, Tricia.

Kris and I had unprecedented access to LeBron and the team. Well, Kris' project later turned into a full-length feature film called *More Than A Game* that my wife and I had the pleasure of watching at the premiere during the Toronto International Film Festival. The movie was absolutely amazing. In fact, it was so good that it was named first runner up for the People's Choice Award, which went to the best film at the festival.

The movie that beat out *More Than A Game*?

Oscar-winning movie *Slumdog Millionaire*.

CHAPTER 6

ADVERSITY

Athlete Clears Hurdle to Succeed: Buchtel Junior Enjoys Success in Track and Football after Losing Part of Arm

When Dion and Ella Jenkins watch their son, David Jenkins, intercept a pass, or make a tackle, or win the 300-meter hurdles or a relay for the Buchtel Griffins, they can't help but be proud. The Jenkins family also can't help but remember a December day in 1996 that changed the family forever.

Jenkins was in fourth grade at the time. He was at a friend's house and mischievously decided to fool around with the washing machine while it was on the spin cycle. Jenkins reached his left arm into the machine, and . . .

"My bone came right out of the skin," Jenkins, now a junior, said about the incident. "The machine was spinning so fast, it twisted my arm so bad that my veins and arteries just snapped. I went into shock. I really didn't feel it until I got to the hospital."

Imagine being a parent and receiving word from a family friend that one of your children had been involved in a terrible accident at a friend's house. That was the situation Ella Jenkins was in when a friend, who worked at Children's Hospital, called her with the news.

"I'll never forget it," said Jenkins' mother, who works as a secretary at Crouse Elementary. "When I found out what happened, I was completely numb. I was in disbelief. They told me my son had cut his hand completely off."

Doctors performed seven surgeries to try to save Jenkins from losing part of his arm. But to no avail. His arm extends about seven inches from his elbow. The heart-wrenching ordeal the family experienced was unbearable, yet, there was Jenkins, resilient, like most children at age 8.

The first thing he said to his parents when they saw him after surgery was, "I love you guys, and I promise I'll do better in school." Said Ella Jenkins: "David was such an amazing child when this all happened. Once I got to see him. He was at peace and he was never upset with what happened. As long as he was OK, we were OK."

Instead of lying in bed, wondering what the future might hold or feeling sorry for himself, Jenkins wanted to know how soon he could get back on the field.

"That's his character," Jenkins' father said. "He's a very humble person with a big heart and he just wanted to go back doing what he did as a kid before his accident."

The next football season, Jenkins was back with the West Griffins pee-wee football team and the teammates who remembered him before his accident were ready to support him when he returned.

By the time Jenkins reached high school and was competing at the varsity level, his teammates, friends and classmates treated him like nothing happened. He continued to be a solid athlete in high school. During his freshman and sophomore seasons, Jenkins played on all of

Buchtel's special teams. Three games into his junior season, Jenkins broke into the starting lineup as a free safety, where he remained the rest of the season. He even registered two interceptions.

"He's one of the biggest hitters I've seen at defensive back since I've been here," said Claude Brown, who completed his ninth season as Buchtel's coach. "He's not afraid of anything. He has a lot of Griffin heart."

This spring, Jenkins decided to try out for track, the first time he's ever participated in the sport. He's also excelling. His main event is the 300-meter hurdles with a best time of 44.0 seconds.

He also is a member of Buchtel's 400, 800 and 1,600 relay teams. As for handoffs, they aren't a problem. "In the 1,600, David leads off, and in the 400 and 800, he's the third leg," Buchtel track coach John Scott said. "On our relays, the first person has it in their right hand, the second person has it in their left hand, the third person has it in their right hand and the fourth has it in their left hand. We have David in the third leg so he can get the baton in his right hand.

"But outside of track or football, he's a wonderful young man."

Jenkins said despite his accident, his life is as normal as can be. "I'm just like everybody else," he said. "I love playing football and running track, I love being with my friends, and my goal is to play football and run track in college."

It's ambition like that which makes Jenkins such an inspiration.

AUTHOR'S INSPIRATION

David is such a wonderful inspiration for those who think that any disability prevents you from going after your dreams. David proved he could still be an all-state performer in track and that he would achieve his dream of playing college football. He went on to play four years at Ohio Dominican University in Columbus, Ohio, an NAIA school, where he was a three-year starter and all-conference player.

St. V-M Golfer to Play for His Grandpa: State Qualifier Has a Promise to Fulfill to Grandfather, Who Taught Him to Be a Gentleman

"Thank you grandpa for teaching me how to be a gentleman on the golf course. I promise to respect the game of golf like you did and I promise to tee one off for you every time."

That was the last message St. Vincent-St. Mary sophomore Jack Uecker wrote to his grandfather, James Pier, after "Jim" died Aug. 2 at age 71, following a three-year battle with cancer. Uecker loves golf. So did his grandfather, who played at the University of Akron in the late 1950s. The two spent countless hours at Fairlawn Country Club and other golf courses around the area, enjoying the game and each other's company. The love they had for each other and the love for the sport were special.

So as Uecker started the season, there was one thing on his mind: making his grandfather proud and keeping his promise. He remained focused all season, even though his heart was heavy, and he played the way his grandfather taught him. Now Uecker is on his way to Columbus as a Division II state qualifier. He shot a 74 during district play, earning the right to play at Ohio State University's Gray Course on Friday and Saturday in Columbus.

One of the things Uecker is looking forward to is teeing up at the state tournament and knowing his grandfather is looking down on him with his warm, inviting and loving smile. On each ball, Uecker wrote a little "G," for "Grandpa."

"Early on in the season, it was pretty tough for me," Uecker said about dealing with his grandfather's death. "But as the season went on, it got easier because, I knew he was still with me at all times." His mother, Juli Uecker, agreed. "I feel like Dad is watching every round of golf Jack plays," she said. "They shared the same passion for the game."

Excelling in athletics was something that seemed to be destined for Uecker. His father, Keith Uecker, was an all-American offensive lineman at Auburn and played 10 seasons in the NFL (1982-1991), two for the Denver Broncos and eight for the Green Bay Packers. He later coached at the University of Akron.

Juli was a star for the St. V-M basketball team and helped the Irish win state championships in 1979 and 1980. In college, she played for the Miami Hurricanes. She said she remembers when Jack, who has three siblings (Tori, Clayton and Jane Anne) started to fall in love with golf. "Most kids, when they are young, like to sit in front of the television . . . and watch cartoons," Juli Uecker said. "But Jack would sit and watch golf. . . . We lived in Hollywood, Fla., on a golf course (Orangebrooke Country Club) and Jack would sit on the back porch on the seventh hole and count people's strokes all day long. Then he would keep running in and report the scores to me all day. And that was when he was 4 or 5."

That love for the game kept growing inside Uecker. In recent years, he competed in the Good Park Junior Invitational, where he learned to play against quality golfers his age from around the state. Now he's among Ohio's top Division II high school golfers.

Earlier this week, Uecker had lunch at Akron Family Restaurant, near St. V-M, with his mother and St. V-M science teacher Mary Jo Chionchio, who was the girls basketball coach when Juli Uecker played. Chionchio later coached the boys and girls golf teams at St. V-M. Juli Uecker said it was a loving and caring gesture on Chionchio's part to agree to meet and to offer encouragement and advice to Jack.

"She is just an amazing woman and she didn't have to do that," Juli Uecker said. "She just looked Jack right in the eye and helped him get focused for what he's going to experience, and it meant a lot to both of us." Jack said he thinks that he's ready to do his best.

"I'm excited and I know it's only my sophomore year, and I just hope I can do well," Uecker said. "I'll just remember something my grandpa told me before he passed away. He said, 'It doesn't matter what situation you're in. Just be yourself, act like a gentleman and know that it's all for God.'"

AUTHOR'S INSPIRATION

Jack Uecker's grandfather, Jim Pier was an amazing man who loved his family, especially his grandchildren. He loved golf, too. That's where Jack got his love for the game. Before Jack entered high school, he would always be at an area golf course with his grandfather. Then, as Jack got older, he started working at an area golf course as a caddy and doing anything that was asked of him.

One of the things that Jack was hoping was that his sick grandfather would still be alive to watch him play in the state golf tournament. Unfortunately, it never happened. But Jack said whenever he's on the course, he always thinks of his grandfather.

I wrote this article in hopes that Jack could be a model of strength for those who had lost loved ones and needed to find a way to move forward.

Family Matters: Ellet Coaching Duo Fights Cancer Together

Gary Yost considers every new day a blessing—a gift from God. No longer does he take anything for granted. Not his wife of 25 years, Tobi. Not his 80-year-old mother, Jacqualine E. Yost. Not his four brothers—Jim, Randy, Joe and Bobby. And not his "family" in the Ellet community, either.

After undergoing surgery three months ago to remove a large cancerous tumor in his abdomen, the 52-year-old middle linebackers coach for Ellet looks at life differently.

So does his brother, Joe, in his 26th season as head football coach for the Orangemen. When Gary started experiencing health problems, younger brother Joe became one of his caregivers.

"I don't think you can ever underestimate the power of prayer," said Gary Yost, who has worked 29 years for Allstate Insurance as a business consultant. "I had people I didn't even know, even ministers, say that they heard about my condition and prayed for me. There were times when I felt alone, but I found strength through prayer and that put me at ease."

Last February, after shoveling his way out of a snow and ice storm at his home, Yost felt discomfort in his abdomen the next day and saw a doctor because the pain was unbearable. At first, Gary and Tobi, who have no children, thought the discomfort might be a hernia. The diagnosis they received was shocking.

There was a cancerous tumor in his abdomen.

For almost two weeks, Yost waited for instructions from his doctor. "When we were going through that 10-day period, it was emotional because so many things are running through your mind," he said. "All I knew was that I had a large mass in my abdomen and I was thinking, 'Am I ever going to be on the football field again? Will I ever be with the kids again? Will I ever swing a golf club again?' "

As Yost told the story, he was overcome with emotion while sitting in the dank and empty Ellet football locker room. He dropped his head and tried to gather himself. "My wife put her job on hold and was there for me the whole way," Yost said proudly. "She's a real trooper."

Tobi said: "What Gary went through really changes your life. The small things and the material things didn't mean anything to me. I realized that I didn't want my life without Gary. My life is Gary."

Yost had surgery in March at Akron General Hospital to remove as much of the gelatin-like tumor as possible. It had attached itself to his appendix and attacked the outside linings of his large and small intestines.

But Yost was advised to see a specialist in Washington, D.C., to remove the rest of the tumor. So Gary, Tobi and Joe Yost flew to Washington in July and met with surgeon Paul H. Sugarbaker to discuss the procedure.

Joe Yost missed a portion of the football team's preseason camp to be with his brother.

"At Ellet, it's a family affair," he said. "As long as this coaching staff has been together here, it truly is. When I had to be away with Gary, the football program didn't suffer one bit when you have Chuck Shuman, Bob Clark and John Sarver there. They divided up my responsibilities and kept everything organized, and I'm very grateful."

On July 21, Gary underwent a 12-hour procedure at the Washington Hospital Center. In describing the surgery, Joe Yost said that Sugarbaker "opened Gary's stomach, heated up a chemotherapy solution and poured it into the abdominal cavity. He let it stew there for about 90 minutes and then they started peeling the lining so that they could remove the rest of the cancer that was left."

During the operation, Yost had 11 procedures performed and Sugarbaker removed the gallbladder and spleen. For the next six days, Yost would have the solution poured into his stomach via tubes, then every 30 minutes, he would be turned so that the solution would move to different parts of his abdominal area. At the end of the day, the solution would be drained and the procedure would start all over again.

Sugarbaker screens potential patients because the surgery is so invasive that some patients can't handle the shock to the body.

"One thing the doctor told me about the surgery was that before and afterward, it was really important that you have family with you," Gary said. "Tobi would be with me for 12 hours and I knew she was always there. When things would get overwhelming, I would just shut my eyes and touch her hand and it helped me get through.

"Joe also would be with me for 12 hours. My mother came down to visit along with my brother Jimmy and Tobi's sister Geri Ann (Tomcik), who lives in North Carolina. She was an angel."

Tobi added: "My sister Geri was a comfort and she was like a mother to me. Every day she had a small gift for me. Her voice was always a calming voice of reason. She thought a lot about what I was going through and that really helped me stay focused. I'm really grateful for her and for Joe. He was there the whole time and gave me strength."

It took time to recover from all the procedures, but Gary started to feel much better in early September. "I started gaining my weight back and getting stronger," he said. In March, Yost weighed 226 pounds. After surgery in July, he was down to 173. His lower body weight reminded brother Joe of Gary's playing days.

"When he graduated from Ellet, he weighed 155 pounds. He was a walk-on (at Akron). The first time he walked on, he got cut," Joe remembered. "But he got bigger and he came out again and they kept him. The next thing you know, he's a starter. Before it was all over, he was an MVP and captain of the team." Yost is listed in Akron's record book as a football letterman from 1971-74.

After all he had been through, Gary couldn't wait to feel good enough to start exercising. "I'll never forget the first time I got back home. I came up to the track at the school with Tobi to walk. I did two laps and it took me about 20 or 25 minutes. Just the other day, I did two miles in 28 minutes," he said.

Yost missed Ellet's first two games of the season but slowly made his way back to the team. "When people are going through difficult times, it's important to set tangible goals. That way, you have deadlines," Joe Yost said. "Gary wanted to be here for two-a-days but that wasn't possible. He missed the first two games but finally, I let him in the press box when he was ready. I didn't want him on the field until it was the right time. I wasn't going to put him in danger. If someone would've hit him, he would've disintegrated."

Two weeks ago, Gary finally made it to the sideline, and it was a great feeling of accomplishment. "When you come back to the field, it all means more," he said. "You think of the kids more and you want to be closer to them."

After all Gary Yost has been through, the sun now seems to shine brighter. The air seems fresher.

And the warm smiles and the friendly handshakes he gives are more meaningful. "I feel pretty good right now," Gary said. "I just feel really blessed. My heart goes out to those who have had to go through worse than I did because I wasn't given a death sentence."

The entire ordeal gave Joe Yost a new perspective on life as well. "Certainly you look at things differently when you have someone that you love dearly and someone that your whole life revolves around go through something like this," he said. "Because I just couldn't even imagine life without Gary."

AUTHOR'S INSPIRATION

The Yost family has been associated with the Akron coaching community for many, many years. The family members are very humbled and don't like attention drawn to them. I came across this story not by one of the Yost family members, but by an assistant football coach on Ellet's staff. The coach informed me that Gary was seriously ill the previous summer and almost died. But Gary, being the humble person he is, never wanted the story to get out. I felt I had to tell his story of remarkable recovery because he could be an inspiration to others that may have been in a similar situation.

Gary, Tobi and the entire Yost family agreed to allow me to write the story and I was honored, privileged and grateful to them. And the great news is that Gary is healthy and still doing what he loves—coaching high school football.

Players Pass It Forward: Area Students Pitch in to Help Local Church Give Out Food

"You cannot live a perfect day without doing something for someone who will never be able to repay you." UCLA men's basketball coach John Wooden said.

Ask a high school athlete today who is John Wooden and a blank stare probably will be the response. But some of these players do have something in common with Wooden, who was 10 national championships in 27 seasons with UCLA. They share a compassion for others.

Players from St. Vincent-St. Mary and athletes from various Cuyahoga Valley Christian Academy teams decided to think beyond themselves. They wanted to make a difference and extend the holiday spirit to others. They did so by helping pastors at Akron Bible Church prepare and hand out food recently in the parking lot of the church on Brown Street.

"The whole community gets involved, and it's an exciting thing," said Randy Baker, an Akron Bible Church senior pastor. "If love is blind, it really does find its way around. And the high school kids really have a good time because they see how this helps so many people." St. V-M boys basketball coach Dru Joyce II said it was important for his players. "Kids sometimes don't understand how much more important it is to give than to receive," he said. "Anything we can do to get them to understand the joy of giving and to understand something greater than yourself when you're helping families and kids who may not have it as good as you and your family, it's a great thing."

Joyce's varsity and junior varsity basketball teams helped unload trucks filled with produce, and they helped assemble toys for distribution. "I enjoyed this because it was doing something good for somebody other than myself," St. V-M senior center Demetrius Brinson said. "It made me want to keep helping people after I was done." Nick Thomas, a senior forward, thought the same way.

"I learned a lot about how blessed we are and that we should always be looking to help others. I think it's a great experience, especially for some of our younger teammates." Senior guard Jamar Holley added: "This experience really helped me to look at everyone every day in my life and to see if there's something I can do every day to help at least one person."

CVCA athletes and coaches have been involved with the food giveaway for the past five years, thanks to Fred Lester. The 58-year-old is associate pastor and director of the church prison and jail ministry. He had two sons, Damion and Harry, who attended CVCA and wrestled. Damion, a 1995 graduate, was CVCA's first state qualifier in wrestling; Harry (Class of 2001) was a four-time state champ. Both are being inducted in the school's hall of fame this weekend.

Fred Lester was introduced to the church at a difficult time in his life, and he didn't hesitate to share his story so that it might inspire others to change their lives. He was incarcerated in the Richland Correctional Institution in the mid-'90s for aggravated drug trafficking, he said. "I got out of the penitentiary on a Wednesday, and the first thing I did was go to a prayer meeting here at the church, and I made a promise to God that I would go every Wednesday. That was in 1996, and I haven't missed a Wednesday."

Lester is happy to see CVCA athletes return every year to help the church. "It gives them respect and a real perspective on what life is really about," he said. "It's about giving, not taking. I was always a taker in my past life. Once I learned to be a giver, it really turned my life around. "With the 3,000 (total) food baskets we give away, it's a good feeling that burns deep in your heart. It's a gratification, a loving and a caring that's addictive. Once you experience it through the baskets of love, you don't want to quit, and it's a feeling that will last with you for a lifetime. When you get that giving spirit, that's God in all of us."

Everyone involved attended an hourlong inspirational service at the church before the more than 300 recipients were given boxes filled with bread, potatoes, fruit, canned goods and other groceries donated by various companies. "I'm blessed. I really and truly am," Connie Dooley said. She was loading her box of food into her minivan as her 4-year-old son stood beside her. "This means so much to us, and it's just a nice thing that they are doing here."

The CVCA athletes who helped out on this night were juniors Zach Butler (football/baseball), Mark O'Brien (basketball/baseball) and Cody Haggard (football), and sophomore football and basketball players Zak Knettel and Jordan Judd. Coaches Kevin Gross and Mark Eger and CVCA Athletic Director and football coach Ray Carroscia also helped. A few days later, boys soccer coach Jason Spodnik had his team lending a hand.

"This gives us an application for what we're trying to instill in the student-athletes yearlong in our sports programs," Gross said. "We're trying to teach more than just success in sports. It's also about the character aspect and what it really means to care about other people, whether that's your teammate or other people that you don't know who are in need. They have to look outside of just playing for themselves. It's a tangible way to help others."

"This was a growing experience for me," O'Brien said. "It was a great feeling to show some love and care to people who really need it. I always look forward to doing these types of services in the community." Butler added: "Spreading the love was a great feeling for me. I remember going home that night and being thankful and grateful for a warm place to stay and a hot meal. I also was glad to help people in any way I could."

Toward the end of the evening, Jacob Everly, who lives near the church, was standing in the parking lot after receiving a box of food. He was there with his girlfriend, Tiffanny Goodhart; his 7-year-old daughter, Alexus Everly, wearing a cute black cowboy hat; his cousin Allen "Bud" Conrad; and 23-month-old Victoria Everly, who was wrapped snugly in her stroller. "It's just wonderful to see so many people come together," Everly said. "It doesn't matter if you're young or old, black or white, middle class or poor. Just look around and see how great it is for people giving and caring. It brought me and Tiffanny to tears.

"Yes, we're here to get a box of food, but there are so many other people here who need it, too, and there's nothing wrong with that." Just then, those still in the parking lot started to spread out and lock hands to form a prayer circle to give thanks for what they had just received. It was the perfect ending to a perfect day.

AUTHOR'S INSPIRATION

I had a great time writing this story because it came at a time when we all forget about where we come from and we just give without wanting something in return. That's what the Christmas spirit is all about. And to see high school student-athletes put aside their own wants and needs to help those in need was a great testament to the kindness in their hearts.

CHAPTER 7

FAMILY

Central-Hower's Coach Moves to N.C., but Parents, In-Laws, Siblings Follow Him

At 41 years old, Dwight Carter didn't think he ever would leave Akron.

He grew up here, played basketball for legendary coach Joe Siegferth at Central-Hower High School in the 1980s and eventually was the head boys basketball coach for six years. Then in June, Central-Hower closed. Carter and his family had to make a difficult decision. Carter, who had taught health at Central-Hower, was out of a coaching job. He could have stayed in the district as a teacher, but coaching was still in his heart. When he couldn't find a coaching job in the area, he expanded his search.

Carter and his family ended up in Smithfield, N.C., where he is the head boys basketball coach and physical education teacher at Smithfield-Selma High School just outside Raleigh.

"It definitely was a life-changing event and a huge decision," Carter said. "Without the strength and faith from my family, it would have been tough. A lot of people are afraid of change, but change is good."

The love that the Carter family has for each other reaches beyond just one household. When Carter entertained the thought of moving to North Carolina, he met with his parents, his in-laws and his siblings. In a show of solidarity, the entire family agreed to move to North Carolina with Dwight and his family.

Bob and Vincetta Carter, Dwight's parents, are retired and didn't think twice about moving. They have been married for 42 years and graduated from Central-Hower, as did all three of their children. Sure, it was tough to leave a place that they had called home for so many years, but being close to their son and grandchildren was all that mattered. So they sold their house, packed their things and moved to North Carolina.

"The decision was a group thing," Dwight Carter said. "My mom and dad and Mary's mom and dad decided to move down here. My brother (Bill) married Mary's sister, and they are moving down here, and my sister (Karen) and her family will be moving down here as well. Having everyone move down with me helped make the transition a little easier because it gave me strength," Carter added. "I had more people to lean on, and that was important for me.

"We're a close family," Vincetta Carter said. "When Dwight was making his decision, we all supported him. We all discussed it as a family, and I don't think Dwight and Mary would have made the choice if they didn't think everyone would eventually all go with them."

It wasn't as though the family hadn't been through adversity. In 2003, Carter's wife, Mary, battled breast cancer. What helped Mary get through her ordeal was the support of her family. Dwight saw the courage and strength in his wife, and it helped him become a stronger man, a more loving and supportive husband and a patient father to his three children: Gabbie (11), Christopher (9) and Alexis (5).

In essence, Mary's experience helped Dwight appreciate the little things in life.

So making the decision to move his family from Akron to Smithfield wasn't as tough as one might think. "That was one of the key things for me," Dwight Carter said. "Mary wasn't afraid to take a chance because of what she went through. She realizes that life is too short, and so she said, 'Let's do it.' She really spearheaded everything with her courage."

In the past, "I could've never been brave enough to do something like this, but life is too short," Mary Carter said. "This could've been a great opportunity that we lost. And it's great having our parents here. It's like we picked up Akron and moved it here."

As for basketball, Carter's team is 7-15 after starting the season 1-10. But Smithfield-Selma's overall record is misleading. The Spartans have won more games than in the past four years combined. They are tied for fifth in their eight-team league, and the top five teams qualify for the state playoffs. Smithfield hasn't advanced to the playoffs in the past seven seasons.

"The biggest thing that drew us to Dwight was his interview," Smithfield-Selma Athletic Director Mike Joyner said. "We narrowed the search down to four candidates, and we interviewed them all in one day. So when you get to that last interview, you seem like you're repeating questions, but we actually talked to Dwight for two hours.

"We were pulled in by Dwight," Joyner said. "When we took a tour of the campus with him, we really felt like he was the right person for the job and that he could take the program in the right direction."

Still, Carter misses all his friends and former players in Akron.

"My kids at Central-Hower were like my family, and it was difficult to leave them. Leaving those kids behind was very, very hard."

One of Carter's prized possessions is a red, white and blue quilt that a former teacher at Central-Hower made and sent to him as a surprise.

"Emily Parker took all the different kinds of spirit shirts I gave out during the six years and made a quilt out of it," Carter said. "There had to be between 20 and 25 different kinds of shirts, and she had all the teachers sign it for me. It's unbelievable, and it symbolizes all the great memories I had at Central-Hower over the years."

AUTHOR'S INSPIRATION

I first met Dwight years before I became a sportswriter. We were both student-athletes at Youngstown State University. I played baseball (briefly) and Dwight was a basketball player. He was good, a very good point guard but didn't get a lot of playing time. He eventually transferred to a school in Indiana so I lost track of him.

About ten years later, I was working for the *Beacon Journal* when I was covering a high school basketball game. And in the stands scouting was Dwight. We hugged for a long time and it was like we hadn't lost a second of time.

Dwight eventually got the head coaching job at his alma mater, Central-Hower, where he did a great job and was successful. It was great seeing my loyal YSU friend do well and it was also great getting to know his family and vice versa. His wife Mary is a sweet woman, very dedicated and supportive. Dwight took the head coaching job in North Carolina and I was sad to see him and his family leave. But the fact that his family collectively decided to make their more and support him by moving their families down to North Carolina for Dwight was the ultimate family sacrifice.

A Family Affair: Jackson Football Coach Phil Mauro Has No Trouble Looking at Player Ty McNab as a Son—In Fact, He Is

The relationship between Jackson football coach Phil Mauro and two-way starter Ty McNab goes way beyond the football field.

It goes way beyond x's and o's. The two share a special bond, one that Mauro said has enriched his family tremendously.

Mauro, his wife Mary, a school nurse, and the couples' three boys, Kyle (10), Colin (8), and Corey (6), have welcomed McNab (18) into their home. Since June, McNab, a senior at Jackson High School, has been living with the Mauros. McNab is black. The Mauros are white.

"When I mentioned the idea to my wife and kids, they were all very excited, and quite honestly, I didn't think there would be any objections," Mauro said. "It just felt like the right thing to do."

For the Mauros, the right thing to do was to get involved. After moving to Canton from Buffalo with his mother when he was 9, family troubles forced McNab to be placed into foster care. But don't get the wrong impression.

McNab is a hard-working, intelligent, athletic teenager. He's a good student, holds down a part-time job at Donato's Pizza and also plays basketball for Jackson High.

On the field, McNab (6-1, 190) is a starting running back and linebacker for the Polar Bears. Unfortunately, as a youngster, he had to deal with difficult situations beyond his control.

Since age 12, McNab had been living with a family in Jackson—Bill and Michele Jones—so he was no stranger to the community. But in May, the Joneses relocated to Chicago and McNab was caught in a very emotional dilemma. Should he go to Chicago after spending six years in the Jackson school system, or remain behind at Jackson for his senior year?

McNab decided to stay. "We still feel he's a part of our family, and he's an important part of our lives," Bill Jones said. "We miss him and love him very much." That's one of the reasons the Joneses decided to return to Jackson this fall to watch McNab play his senior football season. Both had to take a short leave of absence from their jobs. But the sacrifice has been well worth it.

When the Joneses told McNab they were moving, he said he was really confused. "I didn't want to leave my friends," he said. "This was my home and they were my family." Deep down, Bill Jones knew the best thing for McNab was for him to stay in Jackson with his friends and new family.

Before they moved, Bill and Michele contacted Mauro and the coaching staff at Jackson to let them know of their intentions. That's when Mauro decided to act.

He contacted officials at the Stark County Human Services Department to let them know he and his wife were interested in becoming Ty's foster parents. A hearing is set for later this month that will most likely grant legal guardianship to the Mauros.

"This has been an eye-opening experience on two levels," said Mary Mauro, who grew up in a predominately white neighborhood in Columbus. "I'm beginning to learn, understand and appreciate all cultures thanks to Ty. I was never exposed to different cultures while I was growing up, but I think it's very important, especially for our children, that they do learn to appreciate people for who they are, not the color of their skin."

Skin color has never mattered to the three boys. All they know is that they have a new big brother and that he is a starter for the 4-2 Jackson Polar Bears, who are 3-0 in the Federal League.

"Ty always plays football with us and he does all kinds of other stuff with us," Kyle said. "It's really fun having him around." There's no need to ask the boys to name their favorite Jackson player.

McNab said he knew how much he meant to his little brothers when Kyle introduced him to one of his friends as his big brother. "That made me feel really good. It showed how much they care about me."

Mauro, who teaches physical education, grew up in New York City. Prior to teaching at Jackson, he taught in ethnically diverse school systems throughout the country. He said he has more in common with McNab than people think. "Growing up, I was surrounded by Blacks, Hispanics, all types of ethnic backgrounds," said Mauro, who is Italian. "I know how important it is to be exposed to different cultures.

"I also know how important it is for Ty to have a black male role model in his life, and obviously I can't be that to him. But what I can give him is love, support, understanding and discipline so that he makes the right choices in his life. You can do that whether you're black or white.

"The bottom line is that we really do love and care about Ty."

AUTHOR'S INSPIRATION

The Mauro's were in a position to change a young man's life in a positive way, when they decided to take legal guardianship of McNab. Jackson is a predominately white suburb between Akron and Canton. With the situation that McNab was facing, I thought it was a great gesture on the Mauro's part to bring Ty into their home so that he could finish his senior year of high school with his friends, classmates and teammates, instead of moving to Chicago with the Joneses and having to leave all of his friends behind and meet new ones.

Wrestling Just Like Family: Paonessa Reaches Mat Milestone With Lots of Help on the Home Front

When Ralph Paonessa started his career as a wrestling coach almost 40 years ago, he knew little about the sport. Fast-forward to last week, when Paonessa notched a milestone victory that raised his overall career record to 300-117-5. With his head coaching stints between Hoban and St. Vincent-St. Mary, Paonessa has come a long way.

"I didn't know anything about wrestling," he said. "I played football in high school and wrestled a little in college (the University of Akron), but that was just in intramurals."

Over the years, Paonessa learned to love the sport. He did whatever was needed to become a more knowledgeable coach, which meant reading a lot of books and attending clinics all over the state. When he was ready to perfect some of the (wrestling) moves he learned in the early years of his coaching career, he went to his wife, Nancy. They will be married 40 years this June.

"I remember an old movie where the actor played a high school English teacher who bought wrestling books, then practiced the moves on his wife," Paonessa said, jokingly. "I thought that was ironic, because I was an English teacher and I did the same thing."

Said Nancy: "It was especially funny when I was pregnant carrying all three children and Ralph would practice his moves. He didn't hurt me at all, though, and really, it was fun being involved with the sport, because it has been a part of my life for 39 years."

In talking about his career, Paonessa, 65, reflected on when he became the freshman wrestling coach at Hoban in January 1966. "I was the head freshman coach at the time and the program was in its infancy," he said. "But in the fall of 1966, I was asked to take over the varsity program. At first, I turned it down because I didn't know anything about wrestling. So the athletic director was going to sell the mats to Hower (High School).

"But when I got home that evening, I talked to my wife about it, and I started to think about the kids I saw every day in school who loved the sport, and just felt I couldn't let the program die." Paonessa coached at Hoban from 1966 through the 1979-80 school year. He then went to Woodridge for a year, then to St. Vincent-St. Mary, where he led Irish teams through the 1994-95 season.

Paonessa went back to Hoban in 1995 for five years, then retired, only to return after a one-year hiatus. His first hire was Rich Lann, a 1981 Hoban graduate who had wrestled for Paonessa in high school. "Ralph called me and said the only way he would get back into coaching is if I would come back as an assistant, and I said sure," Lann said. "I love it. We both love the sport, and Ralph goes at it like he did years ago. He'll even get down on the mat with the kids, and he'll go at it like he did back when I was wrestling. He's been a great mentor to me, not just in wrestling, but also in life."

Paonessa said the family support has been tremendous over the years. "The years of coaching have been enjoyable because my family has always been involved," he said. "My daughters (Angela and Amy) kept score and did the videotaping and my son (Fred) wrestled for me at St. V-M."

AUTHOR'S INSPIRATION

I really enjoyed writing this story mainly because Ralph has always been a great administrator to work with and he was always about helping kids. But what amused me was when Ralph told me the story about when he first got into coaching wrestling and that he didn't know much about coaching the sport. He then told me how he would practice moves on his wife, who was pregnant at the time. What a woman!

Traveling Fan's Soccer Team: Persichini Sisters of Walsh Jesuit Have a Long-Distance Fan Club of One—Their Father, Who Works in D.C.

Joseph Persichini is an FBI agent—called an "S-A-C," or special agent in charge. He's based out of the Washington, D.C., field office, but his wife, Joleen, and daughters Kristen and Katie live in Northeast Ohio, and soccer is a big part of his life. Kristen is a top senior player at perennial state power Walsh Jesuit, and younger sister Katie is a junior on the Warriors' team.

"There have been days when Joe will fly into town from Washington in the morning, go to the girls' soccer game, then fly back to Washington later that night," Joleen Persichini said about her husband. Persichini is a 26-year veteran with the FBI, joining when he was just 23.

"Ever since we had the girls and they started playing sports, he couldn't stand the thought of missing a game. I'll fax him the girls' schedule and he'll book his flights around their games. He somehow makes arrangements to make the games," Joleen Persichini said.

Kristen said she and her sister appreciate their father's support. "There are times when my dad will leave work on Friday, drive seven hours home for our game, then leave on Sunday back for Washington," she said. "That has to be hard, but he loves to do it and we love him for that."

When their father is away, Kristen and Katie do things with their mom. "A lot of times, the three of us will rent movies and get some popcorn and just spend time together," Katie said. "I know with my dad being away, it's been hard on my mom."

The 2003 girls soccer season should be exciting for the Persichinis. Kristen is back as a senior leader after having a spectacular junior year. She was a Division I All-Ohio first-team selection last year and earned All-American honors after helping the Warriors to a 19-1-2 record. Walsh lost in the state semifinal game.

"That loss was disappointing but we still proved a lot," said Kristen, who was on Walsh's Division II state-title teams during her freshman and sophomore seasons. "When we won state titles in Division II, people were saying, 'Well, wait until you move up to Division I.'

"We moved up and we were still successful. This year, we're hoping everything comes together," she said.

Kristen is a four-year varsity starter, while Katie has started three years. They play right next to each other and talk throughout the matches.

"Kristen pretty much is a consistent player," Katie said. "She plays the same way all the time. She's always energetic and enthusiastic, she plays hard and goes after every ball. She's like a coach out there."

Off the field, Katie and Kristen are best friends. "We do everything together. We stay up late at night and just talk about everything. It's going to be really hard for me when she leaves next year."

Kristen feels the same way. "We'll always be best friends and since we're so close in age, we've always been close," she said. "Katie has always looked up to me and I take that with great respect."

AUTHOR'S INSPIRATION

I thought this was just an awesome story that involved government intervention, international intrigue and a bit of espionage. Oh wait, that was Austin Powers. Seriously, when Walsh girls soccer coach Dino McIntyre told me about this story, I just thought it was an amazing illustration of how much a father understood what was more important—HIS DAUGHTERS. Sorry Federal Government, my daughters are on the "pitch."

The Tausch Family Always Enjoys Hosting Aeros Players: With Jhonny Peralta, They've Worked to Overcome a Language Barrier

The Tausch family kitchen in their Silver Lake home is equipped with a stove, refrigerator, pots and pans—and, oh yes, flashcards with Spanish and English phrases.

The Tausches have enjoyed being a "host family" for Aeros players for years. But this year with guest shortstop Jhonny Peralta of the Dominican Republic, they temporarily faced a language barrier.

Peralta, 20, doesn't speak much English. Call his cell phone and the voice message is in Spanish. And no one in the Tausch household speaks fluent Spanish. So the Tausch kitchen has become a classroom, where two cultures come together. That's where the flashcards come in.

Tim and Betsy Tausch, with the help of Betsy's close friend Susan Weiss, a former high school Spanish teacher, came up with a plan. Betsy Tausch has words and short sentences in English and Spanish posted on walls throughout the kitchen.

She asks questions in Spanish and Peralta tries to answer in English, reading from the wall. "When Jhonny came to live with us, the very first sentence I wrote down in Spanish was 'Good morning. What would you like for breakfast?'" said Betsy Tausch, who is a kindergarten special education teacher.

"Then, he would try to answer in English, eggs, cereal or pancakes. We communicated like that for a while."

With Weiss translating, Peralta said: "When I first got here, I wasn't too sure about everything, but now, I love having a family and I love eating regular food and having people around all the time. It's very nice." Peralta doesn't drive, so Tausch has to take him to and from Canal Park for games.

"A que hora quieres ir al estadio?" Tausch frequently asks. Translation: "What time would you like to go to the stadium?" Peralta answers: "I need to be at the stadium at 3 o'clock."

"We're starting to carry on conversations more," Tausch said. "It's not easy, but we're both getting better."

Helping make Peralta feel comfortable when he first arrived were Amy Tausch (who will be a junior at Walsh Jesuit High this year), and her older sister, Julie, who will be a senior at DePaul University in Chicago.

"I asked a friend to ask Jhonny how he felt when he first came here and I don't think (Jhonny) was really happy living here," Tausch said. "But Amy and Julie were the spark plugs. They took Spanish in high school, so they could talk to Jhonny better than I could. They really made him feel like part of the family."

The rec room in the Tausches' basement has been converted into a room with two beds. That's Peralta's space. "He's very quiet, and he spends a lot of time down there," Tausch said. Amy Tausch said having Peralta around is like having a big brother.

They play basketball together. They watch television together. They have become close friends.

Amy, who plays basketball and volleyball at Walsh, could care less that Peralta plays professional baseball. "It's normal having players live with us because it's been going on for eight years," she said. "I don't think of them as baseball players. I think of them as family." The Tausch family began being the host of players in 1996, the last year for the Canton-Akron Indians in Canton. Pitcher Mike Matthews, now a reliever with the St. Louis Cardinals, needed a place to live and the Tausches took him in.

Since then, the Tausches have had outfielder Dave Roberts, now with the Los Angeles Dodgers; Travis Driskill, a pitcher with the Baltimore

Orioles, and Reds outfielder Russell Branyan spend time at their home. "It was my husband who actually said yes to all of this initially," Betsy Tausch said. "He's been very supportive."

Tausch said people probably think she's "a nut" for taking in players, but she said it's her nature. She's all about family. Her home also is a place where players' wives and girlfriends stay when they don't or can't travel with the team while the Aeros are on the road.

"I'm a team mom," she said. "When guys are on the road, they have someone to call and what I do is let them know they have a mom and a family while they are here. It's important for the ladies to know that they also are welcome here.

"It's all about being a family. This is a gathering place for everyone. No matter where they come from or where they are going in their careers, they can always come home."

AUTHOR'S INSPIRATION

I met the Tausch Family while I was the beat writer for the Akron Aeros, the Indians' Double-A minor league affiliate. I would always see Betsy and her family sitting in the seats where players' family members always sat and after games in the clubhouse family area.

One of Betsy's daughter's, Julie, was interested in pursuing a journalism career in college at DePaul. Julie eventually did a senior project in high school that involved shadowing me for a day as I covered an Aeros game. Julie knew her baseball and it was a pleasure to have her work along side me. As I got to know the Tausch family, I realized that they always wanted to open their home to these players for the summer who needed a place to stay.

The Tausch's other daughter, Amy, was a tremendous athlete growing up and wasn't yet in high school when the Tausch family housed Aeros players. Once Amy reached high school she became an outstanding basketball and volleyball player at Walsh. She later became the junior varsity volleyball coach at her high school.

Julie graduated from DePaul in 2003 with an honors degree in the honors program within the English Department.

I absolutely believe that Amy and Julie's experience with professional athletes helped them excel in their academic and athletic high school careers.

Hec(tor) of a Good Time: Transplanted Luna Family of Central-Hower Excels in the Game It Loves—Baseball

When Hector Luna sees his sons, Hector Luis, Hector Ismael and Hector Enrique playing baseball, his heart swells with pride. He's a proud man, which is why he gave ALL of his sons his first name.

Hector Luis (senior) and Hector Ismael (junior) were both starters on the Central-Hower High baseball team and Hector Enrique, affectionately called "Bobo" by his mother, Ruglas, just finished sixth grade at Jennings Middle School. He also is a baseball player.

"I was supposed to be dead 25 years ago," Luna said. "I never thought I would have kids, so when we had our first son, I was grateful and I wanted him to carry on my name and I felt the same about my other boys. I wanted all of them to continue the name."

There is a reason why Luna thought he'd never play baseball again. In fact, he thought he'd never walk again. While living in Puerto Rico and playing baseball when he was 25, Luna had a tragic accident on the field.

"We were playing a game and we were being no-hit by the opposing pitcher," he explained. "I hit a ball in the gap to left field and I was pretty quick, so I tried to go for an inside-the-park home run. I slid headfirst right into the catcher's shin guard and snapped my neck." After that play, Luna was paralyzed from the neck down for 2½ years.

Miraculously, he began to regain movement in his arms and legs and after thousands of hours of therapy, he said he's doing much better.

"I can probably use about 60 percent of the right side of my body," said Luna, who is a senior sales representative for Summit Racing in Tallmadge. He deals with world-wide customers who speak Spanish and Portuguese.

"I can't do things like I used to, but I do pretty good," he joked. The Luna household also consists of 7-year-old daughter Ruseliz, twin 3½ -year-old daughters Luz and Lydia, and the matriarch of the home, Ruglas. She remembers the first time her two oldest boys wanted to play baseball.

The family was living in Cayey, Puerto Rico, which is about 40 miles from San Juan. The elder Luna owned a modest fruit stand and worked there every day. "There was a field by my husband's fruit stand and Luis and Ismael were maybe 6 and 7 and they always wanted to go play, but their dad was always working," she said. "So I took them to the field one day and they had a lot of fun."

Hector Ismael admitted that when he first began to play baseball, he wasn't very good. "I was terrible," he said. His older brother couldn't wait to get in a jab. "Yeah, he stunk," Hector Luis said, with a huge smile.

But Hector Ismael got the last laugh.

The two brothers were playing on the same team and were playing in the championship their first year. In the last inning, Hector Ismael came to the plate with the game on the line. "All the parents put their hands over their eyes and prayed," Ruglas joked. "Ismael did not get one hit all season, and now, he had a chance to win the game.

"When the ball came, he hit it far into the outfield and the winning run scored. Everyone started to jump up and down and cheer and I just had tears rolling down my face."

Hector Luna said his three boys all have special qualities on the field. "Everything came natural for Hector Luis," Luna said. "He can play every position, he can switch hit and he can even throw with both hands." Hector Luis, who is an All-City first-team selection as a catcher, led Central-Hower with a .542 batting average, seven home runs and 29 RBI. His main position was catcher, but Eagles coach Jerry Van Norstran said Luna was so versatile that he used him in every position.

"He could play everywhere," Van Norstran said. "He's that good. He has the power and he's very smart. He knows a lot about the game."

Luna said he hopes to play baseball in college, and he's even received some looks from major-league scouts. "Someone from the Cincinnati Reds was here in Akron looking at another player and he saw Hector (Luis) and they want him to come to one of their tryouts," Luna said.

Hector Ismael hit .404 with 10 RBI and three home runs for the Eagles and was a second-team All-City infielder.

"Hector Ismael didn't have the natural ability like his older brother but he worked very hard to get where he is," Luna's dad said.

And Hector Enrique is just as talented.

"I think he'll be better than both of us when he's in high school," Hector Ismael said.

Dad said: "Nomar Garciaparra is his (Bobo's) man. He has the best baseball sense I've seen for a young person and I think that's because he's been around his two older brothers."

AUTHOR'S INSPIRATION

Father Hector is a man who I can relate to because of the love for his sons and baseball. But more than that, I have immense respect for what he has been through and despite his tragic baseball accident, he still provides for his family and instills in them the good old-fashioned American belief that if you work hard in life, you can be successful in everything you do.

CHAPTER 8

THE HUMAN SPIRIT

A Little Bit of Baseball, a Big Dose of Salvation: Copley's Tom Brennan Mixes Giving, Faith

A young man wearing khaki pants, a T-shirt and a Cincinnati Reds baseball cap rode his mule through the streets of Hato Mayor, a small, poor city in the Dominican Republic. He made his way past the dilapidated homes, which were one-room shacks lined up side-by-side. Then he had to navigate a narrow dirt path lined with tropical trees. Finally, in a clearing was his destination—a baseball diamond in the middle of a sugar-cane field.

Tom Brennan of Copley knows the young man's route all too well. Brennan has traveled the same route as a member of a non-denominational, non-profit organization called Meeting God in Mission. The organization, based in Erie, Pa., is made up of volunteers from across the country who travel to South American cities. Members typically spend a week in one of the cities spreading a message through street ministry, revivals and door-to-door meetings. They also help residents build schools and churches, as well as provide medical supplies and offer educational assistance to the people, old and young alike.

Then there are the baseball clinics. Brennan, along with other "M-G-M" members, including some former major-league players or college coaches, conducts daily clinics for the residents. Approximately 300 to 500 players sometimes show up for an all-day clinic, and the level of competition is phenomenal. Brennan said there have been several players from the clinics who have signed minor-league contracts over the years.

All of the equipment used during the clinics is donated by M-G-M members or the organization's supporters. "I was so immersed in Tom's stories about his trip," said Jeff Sheeks of Akron, who is one of Brennan's close friends. "He practically had tears in his eyes when he talked about the kids he met. Before he left for his trip, he would go around to his buddies asking them to donate anything they could. It makes you think about how well we have it and how we should never take anything for granted."

Sheeks was moved so much by Brennan's stories that he will be making a mission trip with M-G-M this year. Brennan already is receiving equipment for his next trip to the Dominican Republic, which will be in January. "All of the kids and young men who come to our camps really dream of making it to the major leagues," Brennan said. "They come from really poor towns, and they know the only way out is playing baseball. They come here and they work extremely hard and you can tell they are so grateful that we're spending the time with them."

The players who participate in the all-day clinics are serious about baseball and will do anything to improve their game. A few players even came up with a unique idea for a makeshift batting cage. They took some fishing net, tied it loosely between two palm trees, then took turns hitting balls into the net.

Brennan remembers a young player, age 12 or maybe 13, who was wearing white, pin-striped baseball pants, an oversized Brett Favre jersey that he received from M-G-M, a Nike ballcap and a batting glove. At the end of the day, Brennan went over to the boy and handed him an old baseball. The look in his eyes is something Brennan will never forget.

"This young kid was so happy and proud to get that ball, it was like he received gold," Brennan said. "It was just a great feeling for me because it symbolized how something that we view as minor can make the biggest difference in a kid's life. Every time he picks up that ball, or plays with that ball, he'll think of the people who came there to help him, the people who cared about him and all the other people we met along the way."

Jim McDonald is a former athletic director at Edinboro University and a basketball coach in Erie, Pa., who founded M-G-M in 1994. "The poverty in some of the cities we visit is indescribable," McDonald said. "You see kids who are starving to death or kids who are homeless, but to them, that glove or that hat or that shirt means the world to them. It's like giving someone here a brand new car, and they are so grateful for anything you give them." Some kids come from as many as 30 miles away from the nearest paved road. Their means of transportation is walking.

"I've had a lot of success in my life, received a lot of honors and had lots of opportunities but I've never experienced anything like these mission trips," McDonald said. "To be able to bring doctors, nurses and $3 million worth of medical supplies and to use baseball as a way to help and share the most important thing in life . . . nothing can even come close. It's the greatest opportunity I've ever had in my life."

At the end of the baseball clinics, M-G-M members hold a prayer service with the players. They sit in the stands, if the field has them, or sit right there on the field.

"We share a message about the word of the Lord and it's very interesting because what happens is that people who didn't even participate in the clinic will come over to worship with us," Brennan said.

For Brennan, his trip to the Dominican Republic was spiritual, inspirational and put his life into perspective. Brennan and his wife of 13 years, Jackie, have four children: Ryan (12), Sarah (9), Christopher (5½) and Daniel (2). Brennan said he counts his personal blessings. "My family has been very loving and supportive in what I'm doing and I appreciate them more and more every day," he said.

AUTHOR'S INSPIRATION

Tom was just like me—a baseball fanatic. And so were his young kids. At the same time, Tom was a very caring, loving and giving man. A true Christian. He was well off, but grounded. He lived in a magnificent suburban neighborhood and I remember pulling in his driveway somewhat intimidated. That was until Tom and his wife and kids greeted me in the driveway. I felt completely comfortable.

Tom took me around the back of the house so that I could enter through the kitchen. That's when I noticed it! The dents in the siding of his house. They were the exact size of, let's say, a BASEBALL. It was obvious that Tom's boys used their spacious backyard as a neighborhood sandlot field and the back of Tom's house was homeplate.

Once Tom and I went inside and we talked about why he made the trip to the Dominican Republic, that's when I knew he was a man of outstanding character. Tom was an ambassador in many different ways. He was a Christian ambassador, spreading the word of the Lord to those who prayed and worshipped just like him. And he loved the great game of baseball.

In Their Own Class: Good Model for Student-Athletes

Like any mom, Cindy Doroba always thought her daughter Ann Marie was a special person. "When Ann Marie was about 3 or 4, one of her day-care teachers called me and wanted me to come in and look at her drawings," Cindy said. The teacher told Cindy that the drawings were special. "To me, they just looked like little kids' drawings, but later, we both realized that she was really special."

Now all grown up, Ann Marie just finished her senior year at Woodridge High and after starring in both cross country and track and ranking

No. 2 in her class, she is the 2003 *Beacon Journal* Scholar-Athlete of the Year. In the fall, she will be going to college at Columbia, where she'll be on the track team as a high-jumper.

This year, she carried a 4.046 cumulative grade-point average and was salutatorian of her class. She also attended the University of Akron, taking post-secondary classes before returning to Woodridge for the latter part of the school day.

In sports, Doroba earned three letters in cross country and four in track. As a junior, she was the Division II state runner-up in the high jump (5 feet, 2 inches) and also holds the school record at 5-6, set last year. As a senior, Doroba battled a back injury but still was able to win the Division II district track tournament title.

However, she struggled at the regional and didn't get a chance to go to state. "I always like to be first in everything I do and failing would devastate me," she said. "That's why I was so disappointed with my season this year. But I'll get my rest, and I'll be ready next year."

Doroba recalled how she got started in track. "When I first saw someone high jumping, it looked like fun so I tried it and I loved it," she said. "But when I first started, I was horrible. I got better and in the seventh grade, I won my first meet and that's when I knew this was something I really wanted to do."

Aside from school activities, Doroba has been involved with numerous organizations, including Junior Leadership Akron, the St. Hilary Youth Group and as a volunteer for the Metro Parks Fall Hiking Spree. She works between 15 to 30 hours a week at a clothing store called The Wet Seal Inc. as a sales associate, and she also has done some modeling locally.

Doroba downplayed her modeling ability. "It was nothing big," she said. "I did a fashion show at the Rock and Roll Hall of Fame for vendors from Cleveland."

Asked if she would ever consider a career in modeling, Doroba said: "If the opportunity came up, I probably would. But I'm 5-8, so I'm on the shorter end of the modeling scale.

"My mom is my inspiration," said Ann Marie. "She's a single mom and she always pushed me to do my best. She works in Cleveland and during the school year, she would get up at 5 A.M. and wouldn't get home until 7:30 at night. I really admire her. With everything she has to do, she keeps me focused on my responsibilities."

Said Cindy Doroba: "I never really had to push her. She received so many accolades over the years and she's done it all on her own."

Woodridge Principal Phil Hatton said he has been amazed at how Ann Marie juggles so many activities. "Ann Marie is one of those people who has so much going on, but somehow manages to get everything done and excel in what she's doing," Hatton said. "She excelled in athletics, she excelled in academics and all the while, she's very down to earth. She's one of the most pleasant, polite and friendly people you'd ever want to meet in your life, and we're very proud of the fact that she's going to Columbia. That's remarkable."

"I'm just truly blessed," Cindy Doroba said. "I've been blessed with two wonderful daughters and they both are special."

Ann Marie's 15-year-old sister, Kristin, was a freshman at Woodridge in 2002-03 and also ran track. Kristin said she was happy she had a chance to be on the same team with her older sister, even if it was just for one season. "She really made me work, but it was a lot of fun," Kristin said. "She has done some amazing things."

Ann Marie said she wants to pursue a career in corporate law or business when she starts her academic career at Columbia, an Ivy League school. "I had other offers to run track but I couldn't give up this opportunity," she said.

AUTHOR'S INSPIRATION

Toward the end of the school year every year, the *Beacon Journal* gives out the Student-Athlete of the Year award, which goes to a young individual who meets certain criterion like accomplishments in academics, athletics and community service. We get so many outstanding nominations from school administrators but when I read Ann's submission I was blown away.

I covered Ann in high school so I knew she was an exceptional athlete. I never knew she was even better as a student. I always knew she would go on to do great things because she wanted to have a career in fashion and she did. She had a solid athletic career at Columbia and she later became a model and worked for Macy's in Manhattan. Her high school coach, Jeff Howard, said she regularly hangs out in the Hamptons on Long Island with celebrities. All I can say is that I'm not surprised. She was always focused on what she wanted to do with her life.

Reputation Precedes Garfield's Boys Coach: Chapman a Proven Winner at All Levels of the Game

The Garfield boys basketball team has a new coach with stellar credentials. The new coach, who was approved during last night's board of education meeting, helped St. Vincent-St. Mary win back to back basketball state titles in 1979 and 1980. The new coach helped Ohio State win four consecutive Big Ten titles and was an All-Big Ten honoree three years in a row. And the new coach is a member of the Summit County Sports Hall of Fame.

In new Garfield coach Carla Chapman, the Rams definitely have a coach who knows what it takes to win. "I'm very happy that everything is official and I'm ready to get things started," said Chapman, who is a social service specialist for the Akron Public Schools.

Chapman coached the Rams girls program from 1998-2001 and was named City Series Coach of the Year in 2001. "I was coached and taught by some of the best coaches in the country and I've been able to draw my coaching knowledge from that," Chapman said.

Juli (Pier) Uecker was Chapman's teammate at St.V-M, when they helped the Irish to a 51-0 record in their final two seasons. The two have remained close friends for years. "Carla has just done one amazing thing after another since I've known her," said Uecker, who starred at Miami (Fla.) after her high school days were over. "If there's any female who can run a male basketball program it would be Carla. I'm very proud of her and I know she'll do a great job."

AUTHOR'S INSPIRATION

Carla was a trailblazer in that she didn't care what others thought or what critics would say about her coaching a high school boys varsity basketball team. To her, gender shouldn't have ever been an issue, and she was right; it wasn't. She was a solid coach and she knew the game just as much as any of her male counterparts.

Putting Value of Education First, Foremost

While watching the King James Classic on Saturday, I ran into a delightful, very educated and very engaging man. His name is Jason Mickens and he's from Pittsburgh. During our conversation, Mickens told me he had two sons, 17-year-old Lucas and 14-year-old Ben, who were participating in the tournament with their respective teams. Mickens spoke proudly of his sons' stats on the court. But he told me he wants more from them.

"I want them to go to an Ivy League school," Mickens emphatically said. "Anywhere is good, but that's all I want, for them to go to an Ivy League school."

Mickens is a lawyer. As a youngster, he knew how important education would be for him if he wanted to be successful in life and he worked hard in the classroom.

That conversation I had with Mickens led me in a different direction. Instead of going around asking who is the best player on the court, I wanted the players and college coaches who are in town for the tournament, to reflect on their perspective on the importance of education, as it relates to being a student athlete.

Tommy Amaker, a former Duke star, is now the coach at Harvard. He earned a quality education at Duke and is now coaching at one of the most prestigious universities in the country. Amaker said he wanted to get the message out to student-athletes that education is what matters, more than points and rebounds.

"There's no question that we're in the business of education," Amaker said. "I know coaches like myself still consider ourselves as teachers and educators. At the forefront, we're trying to instill the importance of higher education and the fact that the opportunities they may have by possibly using basketball to pay for their education is a heck of thing."

North Carolina State University coach Sidney Lowe won a national championship in 1983 while playing for legendary coach Jim Valvano as a guard. The Wolfpack upset favored Houston on the last play of the game. Lowe went on to play in the NBA, then was an assistant with the Cavaliers and was coach of the Minnesota Timberwolves and Vancouver/Memphis Grizzlies before taking the coaching job at his alma mater.

Lowe's advice to student-athletes was poignant. "Don't short-change yourself," Lowe said. "Take care of your business so that when you're ready to go to college, you don't have to worry about a college choosing you. You can choose what college YOU want to go to."

As I made my way around the basketball courts, I noticed a tall young man dribbling a basketball alone. He was getting himself psyched up for his next game. His name is Wally Judge, from Jacksonville, Fla. For some reason, Judge, who is 6-foot-9 and has committed to Kansas State, looked like an interesting person. So I walked up to him, interrupted his dribbling and introduced myself. I started asking Judge questions about where he was from, how his high school team did this past season and what he averaged. He said he averaged 17 points and 11 rebounds a game at Arlington Country Day. Impressive statistics to me.

So after talking to Mickens, Amaker and Lowe about the importance of education, I decided to ask Judge for one more extremely important stat, his grade-point average. He replied, "It's a 3.8." Judge took a business law class in school this year and is interested in studying law in college. Judge gets it. And maybe he'll follow in Mickens' shoes.

AUTHOR'S INSPIRATION

Often times, student-athletes forget the most important thing—being a student. They think their abilities will overcome any academic shortcomings they may have. It's a tough lesson that some learn the hard way.

During the popular King James Shooting Stars Basketball Tournament, which draws more than 500 teams from all across the country to Akron, I was looking for a story, and not just, "Who is the next LeBron James?" I decided to make the athlete issue LESS of an issue and focus on the student—a student. That person happened to be 6-9" Wally Judge. He was quick to point out all of his statistics on the court and that he was a Kansas State recruit. But when he told me his grade-point average, I figured he had his head on straight.

'Superstar' Song Motivates Athletes to Reach for Goals

In my musically inclined family, I played (briefly and badly) the piano, clarinet and snare drum.

There are those in my family, however, who have done well in the field. My mother is a former gospel recording artist. My younger sister is a classical pianist with her master's degree in classical piano from Howard University. She appeared on *Showtime at the Apollo* with host Steve Harvey and finished second, which is an amazing feat, considering she played a classical piece and didn't get run off the stage by Mr. Sandman.

I tell you all that so you understand music always has been an important part of my life. So recently, I was listening to a song by Lupe Fiasco called *Superstar*. The catchy lyrics of the chorus are:

"If you are,
What you say you are,
A Superstar.
Then have no fear . . .
The crowd is here,
And the lights are on,
And they want a show oh oh oh, yeah."

This song has been played on major television networks before NBA and college basketball games. The lyrics, about having fear and overcoming it to perform at a high level, illuminate what motivates so many top athletes. Think about those words and imagine how they can inspire a high school athlete. So what do the lyrics mean to some of our area's best athletes? Ten "superstars"—student-athletes who won a state championship this season or were named Player of the Year in their respective leagues—gave their opinion.

Leanna Hoover, Firestone, Senior, Diving

"Star" Status: Won the Division I state diving championship this past season, becoming the first Firestone diver to accomplish the feat. And talk about fighting through fear, this young lady faced fear head on. Two days before the district meet, she stepped on a needle and as she tried to remove it, half of the needle stayed in her foot. She had to undergo surgery to remove it just days before competition, and despite competing through excruciating pain, she persevered and eventually reached the top.

Comment: "To me, that song means that if you go into any situation with a positive attitude, you can make anything happen. You can accomplish anything if you tell yourself you can. As far as the fear part, well,

I looked at it like this: It was my senior year, it was the last chance for me to prove to my friends, family, classmates and my competition what I could do. And to be honest, having that surgery before districts in a way was the best thing that ever happened to me. I was nervous going into the meet and it was the hardest thing I've ever done. But looking back, I felt if I could finish third at districts with my injury, then I could accomplish anything at state, so that inspired me."

DeVonne Howard, Orrville, Senior, Track

"Star" Status: Won the Division II state championship and set the state record in the long jump with a jump of 19-7¾ which was the longest jump in any of the three divisions.

Comment: "Long jump to me is a way to express myself and to display my talent. Making it to state was an accomplished goal. I was determined and I had no fear because with God nothing is impossible. It was like, 'lights, camera, action' when I took my last jump. Next, I was on the podium as my name was being announced. Superstars are not a dime-a-dozen. To be a superstar requires hard work and dedication. If you want the spotlight, how hard are you willing to work?"

Shamira Marshall, Nordonia, Senior, Golf

"Star" Status: A Kent State recruit, Marshall was the *Beacon Journal* girls Golfer of the Year the past two seasons.

Comment: "If you keep working hard, you can get to that level of superstardom, where everyone wants to watch you. I try to make fear a positive thing. Like, it's a good thing that people are watching you. So you have to stay focused because they came here to see you."

Ramel Mitchell, Firestone, Senior, Basketball

"Star" Status: A first-team Division I All-Ohio player who was the City Series Player of the Year the past two seasons and is the school's all-time leading scorer.

Comment: "The lyrics and the song are self-explanatory. If you feel you're the best, then go out and prove it without being cocky. Be confident and don't worry about failure. Just do your best to be the best because faith without hard work—you're done—so if you realize that and believe in yourself, you can achieve anything you put your mind to."

Brittany Orban, North Canton, Senior, Basketball
"Star" Status: Northwestern University recruit was a three-time first-team Division I All-Ohio selection and a three-time Federal League Player of the Year.
Comment: "I always try to hold a humble nature about myself, so saying that you're a superstar truly isn't necessary. As for fear, if you've worked extremely hard to gain the success that you've had, then you shouldn't have any fear because what you've done over and over and over a billion times should come as second nature to you."

Donny Roys, Medina, Senior, Cross Country
"Star" Status: Division I cross country state champion last fall.
Comment: "The song means you can't go into any race or any competition nervous and uptight about it. If you do, then you're bound to fail. You have to act like you're 'all that,' but not in a cocky way. In a confident way. You have to be humble but know that you have to go out there and just take care of business."

Chase Skonieczny, Walsh Jesuit, Senior, Wrestling
"Star" Status: Kent State recruit won the Division II 135-pound state championship in February and a month later won the national championship at a tournament in Virginia.
Comment: "That song means if you believe in yourself, then the sky is the limit. If you're focused and you believe in yourself, then you never have anything to worry about."

Terrence Somerville, Buchtel, Senior, Track

"Star" Status: University of Cincinnati recruit broke Ted Ginn Jr.'s state record in the 60-meter hurdles at the state indoor meet in February.

Comment: "When I hear that song, it says to me that everything you need to be the best and to be successful is right here in front of you. Like the song says, if you claim to be the best, if that's what you claim to be, then you just need to be confident, go out and do it, and go out and prove it."

Elizabeth "Georgia" Stokes, Hudson, Sophomore, Softball

"Star" Status: As a freshman, went 2-for-3 and drove in two runs in the Explorers' 4-0 win against Elyria in the Division I state championship. Family moved to area from Atlanta during her eighth-grade year, thus earning her the nickname "Georgia."

Comment: "Those lyrics are inspirational because it makes you believe in yourself. For me, going into our games with your teammates all around you, it gave me a lot of confidence, so you felt like you could accomplish anything and overcome anything as long as you had your teammates there with you."

Danny Thompson, Cuyahoga Valley Christian Academy, Senior, Soccer

"Star" Status: First-team Division II all-state performer who helped the Royals win the state championship this past fall. A Messiah (Pa.) College recruit.

Comment: "When I think of those lyrics, I think about how there are so many pressures as an athlete we feel, and I think of Psalms 46 that starts out: 'God is our refuge and strength, a very present help in trouble, therefore will not we fear, though the earth be removed, and though the mountains be carried into the midst of the sea . . . be still, know that I am God.' As a Christian, I find so much peace in that verse because with all the chaos around me, I can calm down because of the peace (God) gives me. My strength is not by my own power, so I feel humbled every time I step on the field with my teammates because there's a bond—a bond that goes way beyond winning a state championship."

AUTHOR'S INSPIRATION

Music always inspires the soul. The rhythms and the beats stir us, especially athletes. At every level of competition, you can find players tuning themselves out from the rest of the world and tuning into their own world of music with their iPods. It's their way of getting pumped up for the big game.

The music could be hip-hop, country, classical, heavy metal, it doesn't matter. All that matters is that the music inspires you. Recently, a pop song hit the charts that you couldn't get out of your mind. High school students, regardless of their background, were listening to it constantly. I decided to ask 10 student-athletes about what that song and the lyrics meant to them—to see why it stirred them.

Buchtel, Yale Mold the Lives of Two Teammates: Kirk, Manley Treasure Educational Experience

It has been a time of fond football memories for two former Buchtel stars, Bill Kirk and Phil Manley. This year's Griffins are headed into the state regional finals this week. And Kirk and Manley were happy, too, to be a part of a celebration last weekend in New Haven, Conn., of great teams they played on while college students at Yale.

Yale was celebrating having become the first football program in the country to record 800 wins. Kirk and Manley played there in the late 1970s and early '80s as the school compiled a record of 26-4 from 1979 through 1981, including three-consecutive Ivy League championships. The 1980 and 1960 championship teams received special recognition during halftime of the Yale-Princeton game.

Manley, who graduated from Buchtel in 1977, was Yale's first black starting quarterback and Kirk (Buchtel '78) was a defensive lineman. "They were both great young men and both had a great sense of humor. They kept the team loose," said legendary Yale coach Carm Cozza, who coached the Bulldogs for 32 years and is the school's all-time winningest coach. "Phil was undersized but was a gifted athlete. He was quick on his feet, and he ran the option very nicely for us," Cozza said. "Bill was also undersized for a lineman, but he was very strong and highly competitive. They were two really good kids for us and we were fortunate to get them."

Manley remembers learning to become a strong leader at Yale. At the time, there weren't many blacks on the team, but race was never an issue for Manley at the school. "There weren't many blacks in the Ivy League at all, yet my experience at Yale was one of the best I ever had," said Manley, who lives in Maryland with his wife, Patricia, and their two sons, Carter, 4, and Jordan, 7. Manley is an account executive for Baxter Healthcare Corp. "I was going to one of the top schools in the country for an education and for athletics and color was never an issue," Manley said.

Kirk admired Manley not only for his athletic prowess but for his character. "Phil didn't know anyone when he arrived at Yale, and the adjustment was difficult," Kirk said. "The academic demands at Yale combined with the time and physical commitment of playing college ball can be daunting. Phil paved the way for me at Yale. He took care of me and took me under his wing. It was almost like a big brother thing. He was even the best man at my wedding." But as proud as the two are to be Yale graduates, they are even prouder of their Buchtel connection. If you walk through Kirk's West Akron home, you'll see pictures of him and his teammates from Buchtel hanging on the wall, or on his desk in his Florida room or posted on the refrigerator.

He wants everyone to know where he came from and who his friends are—whether they are black or white. Kirk is a Griffin for life and makes sure he attends a few Buchtel football games a year with his daughter Lyndsey, son Miles and wife Kathy, a 1980 Firestone graduate. "The

Buchtel experience was great," said Kirk, a recruiter for an information technology firm. "It was as good as it gets. There were no agendas and friendships were based on trust. Attending Yale was an unbelievable opportunity. Despite all the privileged backgrounds of the students at Yale, I felt Phil and I were better rounded individuals than most 'Yalies.' Buchtel was a big part of that feeling."

Even though the Kirks and Manleys live in different states, both families remain close and see each other three to four times a year. "It's a priority," Kirk said.

Kirk remembers his years at Buchtel as a time of personal growth and learning a solid work ethic. Buchtel was an unusual situation for Kirk. He was in the minority, which didn't matter to him. "Buchtel was known more for its athletics than academics, but we had advanced placement classes and the students and teachers were excellent," he said. "I took advantage of the AP classes and never felt short-changed (academically). I surrounded myself with quality people like (former Buchtel coach) Mike Buckner. He was the one who got me to play football."

Buckner, now the athletic director of the Akron Public Schools, coached football at Buchtel from 1971 to 1978, compiling a 46-28-2 record. He is the only black coach to be inducted into the Ohio High School Football Coaches Hall of Fame. Another Griffins player who went to an Ivy League school was Ron Mosley, who played at Brown.

Buckner said Kirk and Manley were two of the best he ever coached because of their work ethics. "Bill was interesting in high school because he was a basketball player and had never played organized football," Buckner said. "I saw him in the hall one day and I told him he would be a better football player because he was a hard worker. He came out as a junior and started for me. And Phil was the best quarterback I ever had," Buckner said. "Those two guys represent Buchtel very well, and I'm proud of what they have accomplished in their lives."

Manley's memories of his days at Buchtel reveal enthusiasm and love for the school and the people who influenced him. "Buck was one of the great people I've met in my life," Manley said. "I view him as a father figure. He was one of the first people to push me beyond what I could do. There weren't many black men around in his capacity so he was someone I admired and looked up to," Manley said. "To this day, when I face a difficult situation and have to perform, I envision him in the audience and he will not allow me to fail."

Manley treasures the friendships he made, too. "No doubt about it, my best friends in life are the ones I went through high school with, like Bill," Manley added. "Even though college was great, the greatest influences in my life were teachers from Buchtel like Mrs. (Tina) Mogen, Mr. (Carl) Hale and Mr. (Bill) Holko. They had a lot of confidence in me. They were passionate about what they did and they gave more than what they received. I walked out of Buchtel with all the confidence a human being could have at that stage in life."

AUTHOR'S INSPIRATION

I've known Bill Kirk for a long time because our kids went to the same school, St. Sebastian. In conversation, Bill would always talk about how proud he was of the fact that as a white man, he graduated from a predominantly all black high school in Akron. He said the experience was priceless because he learned to understand the black culture and embraced it, just as much as he embraces his white culture.

Bill was an outstanding athlete at Buchtel in football and basketball and earned a football scholarship to Yale. His best friend and teammate, Phil Manley, who is black, also earned a scholarship to Yale and was the Bulldogs' first black starting quarterback. When I came up with the idea to write this story, I wanted to get across the message that it didn't matter where you came from or what your background was, if you worked hard in everything you did, you could go to the best schools in the country, like Bill and Phil, and a man named Barack.

From Backboards to Blackboards: Nate Schindewolf Scores Plenty of Points for Akron, and He Makes It a Point to Care Plenty for the Students He Teaches

No matter where life takes Akron Zips basketball player Nate Schindewolf, or what challenges he faces in the future, he'll never forget his experience as a student-teacher at Coventry High School. The people he met always will have a special place in his heart.

Schindewolf, an education major, spent two months with students who have learning disabilities. He worked with long-time Coventry special education teacher Ron "Pops" Dula. A visitor to their classroom would notice that the students take a little more time to express themselves. But they are bursting with love and kindness, especially when there's a relationship with someone such as Schindewolf as their teacher.

One day last week, Schindewolf went back to the school to substitute in the computer lab. His former students knew he was in the building and were waiting for him to make a visit. During lunch period, he visited his old classroom and was mobbed near the doorway. He was showered with hugs and slaps on the back. It was obvious that the students love Schindewolf—and that the feeling is mutual. "This is the best feeling in the world," said the soft-spoken, mild-mannered Schindewolf. "It doesn't matter how bad of a day I've had, these kids always pick me up."

The students—Worthy "Ben" Rafferty, Brothers Joseph and Rick Andrews, Jim Minnick, Katherine Eubanks, Brandon King, Brian Guinther, and Bill Gill.

These aren't just names of students. These are the names of students who have filled Schindewolf's heart with joy.

"It's exciting to listen to them tell stories about what they did over the weekend or something that happened in their lives," Schindewolf said. "It's important to them, so it's important to me to listen." Each day, Dula, Schindewolf and teaching assistant Cindy Griffis watched their students accomplish feats that most people consider simple, everyday tasks. Such as writing your name.

Guinther has won national awards as an All-Terrain Vehicle (ATV) racer. Sometimes, he has trouble with his speech and, when he gets excited, he stutters a little. When he was asked his last name, Guinther couldn't get it out. Schindewolf suggested that Guinther write his name on the board.

Guinther took his time. He tried to loop the capital "G," but it was backwards. He erased and tried again and again. His last name started to become recognizable.

G.

Gui.

Guint.

Guinther.

When Guinther sat down, he received a round of applause from his classmates—and from Dula, Schindewolf and Griffis. Guinther felt proud that he was able to write his last name. Such small accomplishments cheer the teachers and students every day.

Richard Andrews appreciates how Schindewolf taught him to write in cursive. "He's a super guy, and I'm glad I can write in cursive now," he said. King loves the magic trick that Schindewolf showed the class. King didn't understand how Schindewolf made water disappear, but the experiment taught the students about evaporation. Those are memories the students will take with them forever.

Hanging on the door of Dula's classroom is a picture of Schindewolf playing in a game. Schindewolf is driving past an opponent to the basket. Dula got the picture off the Internet the same day that Schindewolf was named Mid-American Conference Player of the Week.

"I had no idea he got the award," Dula said. "He never told anyone about it. The day I found out, I said: 'Nate! Did you forget to tell me that you were the MAC Player of the Week?' He said, 'Oh, yeah, sorry.'"

"He's just a very modest person, and he doesn't want to be known as a basketball player. He wants to be known as a good teacher who cares about his kids.

His students haven't seen him play, but they talk about him as if he were an NBA star. "They know I play, but they don't know the extent," said Schindewolf, a guard who is the Zips' leading scorer this season with a 15-point average. "It's funny that they think I'm this great basketball player."

Schindewolf incorporated basketball in his lesson plans. He devised a game in which he asked the students questions and, if they get the answer right, he allows them to shoot baskets. He would draw a backboard on the chalkboard, then set up a waste can against the chalkboard as the basket. The students would shoot from different spots in the classroom and get points.

"Joe is the king of hoops in here," Schindewolf said.

Someone commented that maybe Akron coach Dan Hipsher could use Joe Andrews on the team. King jumped in and asked, "Who's Hipsher?" Schindewolf broke up in laughter.

Schindewolf's day as a teacher started early and ended late. He would arrive at Coventry just before 7:15 A.M. and leave at 2:45 P.M. Then, he went right to Rhodes Arena for practice.

"The drive-time from the school to the gym is very important for me," he said. "That's when I can just relax and be by myself for like 10 minutes or so. While I'm driving to practice, I get in my basketball frame of mind. If I've had a bad day at practice, just being with the kids puts everything into perspective, because they're always in a cheerful mood, and it seems like they never have a bad day. They make the most out of each and every day. I am very busy with everything, and it's made me more disciplined in a lot of the things I do," Schindewolf said. "But right now, I feel like an old man. I'm ready to go to bed around 9 P.M every night."

The importance of education is something Schindewolf learned long ago. His father, Gene, has been a physical education teacher and boys basketball at Manchester for 16 years. He's also the athletic director. "Seeing how my dad interacted with his students over the years had a big impact," Schindewolf said.

Schindewolf's uncle, Ron Graves, is a vocational evaluator for the Akron Public Schools. The rest of the Nate Schindewolf's family consists of his mother, Kathy, and younger sister, Nela. Gene Schindewolf said, "I'm fortunate both Nela and Nate have their mother's brains."

Dula, Schindewolf and Griffis have a unique, family-like relationship with the students. For the students, the classroom is their home away from home. They care about each other and they want to help each other succeed. For the teachers, nothing is more important than making the students feel special. Dula said that part of being a good teacher is gaining the trust and respect of your students. Schindewolf earned that respect because he totally committed himself to his students, Dula said.

"The kids can tell Nate isn't a phony, and it comes through in his teaching. He isn't just here to get his student-teaching out of the way. He is genuinely interested in the kids," Dula said. "He really wants to help them out and make their futures brighter, and the kids idolize him. You need a lot of patience and compassion, and Nate has it. There's really not a lot I can't say about him."

AUTHOR'S INSPIRATION

For Nate, there was no other occupation after graduating from the University of Akron. His dad was a longtime teacher and coach so this was a no-brainer for Nate. I was covering the University of Akron athletics at the time Nate was a senior basketball player and doing his student teaching with special education students. When I followed Nate around for the day, he was great at his job, if you want to call it a job. It wasn't work for him. You could tell it was fun and that he enjoyed being with the students, who were indeed special people.

Nate was patient, caring, understanding and you could tell he was going to be a great teacher. Nate wanted to know more about his students. They wanted to know more about Nate as a basketball player, which made him uncomfortable. He didn't want to feel like he was special. Basketball was just a vehicle that put him in his students lives. He was more interested in letting his students know that he felt they were just as special to him as they thought he was to them.

Mikenna Racing the Long Run: Fleet-Footed Freshman Earns Regional Shot Despite Illness

Heading into the Division I girls district track championships last Saturday at Kent Roosevelt, Stow freshman distance runner Mikenna Stephenson could've crumbled amid the pressure of competing in such a big race at such a young age. She's only a freshman, after all.

But Stephenson is and always has been a fighter. A competitor in every sense of the word. So, as she got herself set for the 3,200-meter finals, she stayed calm and collected. And, in the end, Stephenson finished second with a time of 12:04.7, behind Kent Roosevelt's Kelly Felter (11:24.0) to advance to the regional meet Saturday at Austintown Fitch. The top four finishers in each event advanced.

"I prepared myself for that meet, but I was really surprised at how well I did," Stephenson said. "My goal was to just go out, relax and see what would happen."

Stephenson might have been relaxed, but her parents, Michelle and Ken, were a nervous wreck. "I could hardly sit down," Michelle Stephenson said. "When the race started, we just wanted her to finish. But when she came in second, we were absolutely blown away and thrilled. We were like, 'Where did this come from?' She's come a long way, and there have been some challenges in her life, but seeing her make it to the regionals is one of the greatest thrills for us."

The Stephensons want people to know their daughter as a normal high school student-athlete who does well in the classroom, is active in her church—St. Eugene's Catholic Church in Cuyahoga Falls—and has lots of friends. But Stephenson also has cystic fibrosis, a disease caused by gene defects that prevent cells in the lung and elsewhere from making a key protein. As a result, a thick, sticky mucus clogs the lungs. Cystic fibrosis afflicts about 30,000 American children and young adults.

"One of the things that has always concerned us is that once people know Mikenna has cystic fibrosis, that always becomes the primary focus," Michelle Stephenson said. "We just hope that people treat her like they do anyone else because that's what she wants, to be treated like a normal teenager." Stephenson was diagnosed with cystic fibrosis when she was 7.

"I didn't know what it was," she said. "To me, it was just like someone telling me I had a cold." But once Stephenson turned 10, she began to understand the extent of her disease. It was a very tumultuous time in her life. "I did ask myself, 'Why me?'" she said. "I remember wondering why this had to happen to me." Rather than feeling sorry for herself, Stephenson made a commitment that she was going to beat this thing. That cystic fibrosis wasn't going to control her life. She was going to be in control. So Stephenson fought back and still is fighting.

"Mikenna is a very vivacious young lady, and her family really has tried to give her as much of a normal life as possible outside of cystic fibrosis," said Dr. Greg Omlor, Stephenson's physician and a family friend. "It's important for Mikenna to have something like running to give her life a focus instead of the focus always being on the disease."

Michelle Stephenson said family members and friends have been extremely supportive over the years. "We're very strong in our faith, and everyone at our church has been wonderful," she said.

Stephenson ran cross country during the fall, but it was a disappointing season for her. The weather at the beginning of the season was hot and muggy—terrible conditions for Stephenson to run in. She had to quit before the season ended. "I felt like I let my teammates down," she said. She ended up needing intravenous therapy all through the fall, along with daily medications.

"Typically, it's been like that for Mikenna the last few falls," her mom said. "There's a lot of daily maintenance. But the good news is that there was no special handling this spring. This is the best time of year for her to compete because the weather, for the most part, is cool." And with a regional berth last week, Stephenson said she felt like she redeemed herself. "My goal now is to make it to state," she said. "That would be awesome."

AUTHOR'S INSPIRATION

For anyone who thinks they have it bad, when you think that your day is the day from heck, just think of Mikenna, a young lady who had such a debilitating condition like cystic fibrosis but never let it get her down. She never let the disease keep her from her love of running and competition. When she qualified for the regional tournament as a freshman and once I learned that she did it while dealing with cystic fibrosis, I was a huge fan.

Love of the Game Overcomes Adversity: Only Five Years Removed From Not Having Program, Buchtel Is Improving and Becoming Competitive

There are no City Series championship baseball banners hanging in the Buchtel gym. The Griffins haven't won a game since the 2000 season and they are 0-10 this year. Yet, Coach Steve Deitrick knows a winning team when he sees one.

"We don't get any respect any time we step onto the field," said Deitrick, who teaches astronomy and physical science at the school. "It's very frustrating because our guys work very hard. We've overcome a lot of obstacles, and I'm proud of these guys no matter how we finish the year. They take pride in what they do."

When Deitrick approached then-Buchtel principal Larry Wiegel five years ago about re-starting the baseball program at the school, Deitrick knew it would be a challenge. Before 1998, Deitrick's first year, the school had not had baseball for six years. Deitrick knew he would have kids who hadn't played in years.

Kids who didn't own gloves. Kids who really didn't know the game. "Finding the interest was the biggest challenge," Deitrick said. "Then, we had to deal with the fact that we didn't have a facility or equipment. We basically had to start from scratch. I even had about three kids at the time who couldn't swing and I ended up using those kids as starters because we just didn't have enough players. It was like the movie *The Wildcats*."

Five years later, the Griffins are a baseball team. Forget about their record. They have players who love and respect the game. "This year, we're more baseball sound as a team," Deitrick said "Even though we're 0-10, we've had five games decided by two runs or less, we have a .323 team batting average and we've doubled our run output from last year."

The Griffins have players such as senior catcher Sean Montgomery, one of the team captains who leads the team with a .630 batting average with three home runs and 13 RBI. Montgomery is the first player since 1998 to homer for the Griffins.

"Baseball has always been my first love," he said. "I enjoy it more than any other sport I've ever played." Montgomery was an all-district receiver for Buchtel this past football season. He doesn't like losing; neither do any of his teammates.

Their goal is to play hard, compete every game and earn the opponent's respect. "We try to go out every game and prove that we belong out there," he said. "We're not playing just for something to do. We're baseball players like everybody else."

Montgomery plans to play baseball at Virginia State University next year, and his favorite baseball player isn't Mark McGwire, Sammy Sosa or Barry Bonds.

It's former Negro League star catcher Josh Gibson. "He went through a lot when he played and he showed his true love for the game," Montgomery said. "I admire that."

Buchtel's top pitcher is junior Brandon Williams, who also starts at shortstop. Williams is a tall, wiry kid who's always covered in dust after a game. He leaves everything on the field. "That's the only way to play," he said. "You have to put your heart into the game if you want to feel good about yourself."

Junior first baseman Ashley Dent put the game into perspective. "I hope to play baseball in college," said Dent, who has a 3.4 grade-point average. "And I would love to make as much as Jason Giambi and Derek Jeter, but education comes first."

Added Deitrick: "The most rewarding thing about this job is watching the kids develop and grow physically and mentally. Winning is great, but watching them develop a love for the game is what I appreciate more than anything."

AUTHOR'S INSPIRATION

On the outside, observers could say that Steve looked like a fish out of water. Here was this young, white guy coaching an inner-city high school baseball team with not one white player on the roster.

I played in high school and walked on at Youngstown State University but left the team after two years because of bad grades and general immaturity issues. The point is that I respected Steve and the players for dedicating themselves to the game and the program.

They were at a disadvantage because in this sport, you continually have to develop your skills year round, every year, or you fall behind. This was a program that wasn't even in existence for several years and it basically had to start from scratch.

It didn't matter, Steve and his players loved the game and they wanted to field a team. They didn't care about wins or losses. All they cared about was respecting the game and playing a game that is my all-time favorite sport.

Buchtel's Jones One of the Boys: Senior Girl, Who Is Captain of Boys Team and Its Leading Scorer, Shooting for College Scholarship

Tiara Jones has earned her right to be called a senior captain on the Buchtel boys golf team. That's right, captain of the boys team. Because Buchtel doesn't have a girls golf team, Jones, a transfer from Canton McKinley, where she played on the girls team, is allowed to play on the boys team.

She has proven she can get it done on the golf course, even at an early age.

"I started golfing when I was 3 and I won my first tournament when I was 7 at Clearview Golf Course in East Canton," she said.

Years later, Jones is still on top of her game. She is Buchtel's leading scorer, averaging 45.5 per nine holes, as the Griffins prepare for the City Series championship today at Firestone Country Club Public Course.

Tuesday, Jones participated in the girls sectional tournament at Turkeyfoot Golf Course, where she shot a 43 on the front nine and a disappointing 50 on the back for a final score of 93.

"I had a little trouble on the back nine but that's OK," she said. "I just have to get ready for the City championship." Jones admitted she hoped to do better in the sectional tournament but enjoys playing with other girl golfers. "It goes both ways actually," she said. "I like playing against other girls but I also like competing with the boys because it's a huge challenge. But the main point is that I love golf, so I'll play under any circumstances."

When Jones steps onto the tee box, she isn't teeing up her ball from the women's (red) tees. She's hitting from the white (men's) tees and just letting it rip. "Tiara's strong point is her long game," Buchtel coach Robert Garnett said. "She really smashes the ball. When she steps up to the tee and hits, she gets everyone's attention."

Jones said her longest drive is 298 yards.

Garnett is impressed with Jones' consistency, and he also likes how she stays focused. "She really wants to play in college and she really wants to get a scholarship," Garnett said. "There was a time when a female player could shoot under 100 for 18 holes and get into a Big Ten school. Now, that window is closing and the scores are getting lower and lower. Tiara knows she can improve and she's a hard worker. I know she'll be playing in college somewhere next year."

AUTHOR'S INSPIRATION

It's not too often that you see a girl playing on the boys golf team, let alone being the captain and low scorer. Garnett said he was proud of what Tiara accomplished because at the time she was playing, Tiger Woods was helping change the perception of golf, as far as young, African-Americans were concerned.

Jones went on to play a year in college at Alcorn State before returning home to go to school.

'The Bowl' Games Bowl 'Em Over: City Series Squads Call It Second Home. Past Players Thankful For 'Turkey Day' Play

Whenever Don Sine is traveling around Akron and sees a sign giving directions to the Rubber Bowl, he can't help but think about wonderful times. Sine, a former All-City running back for Garfield in the late 1960s, isn't alone. There are thousands of Akronites with fond memories of the stadium affectionately referred to as "The Bowl."

Sine can describe memories at the Rubber Bowl as if the events happened yesterday. "It just gets my juices going," he said. "I get goose bumps. I grew up in junior high going there and watching Garfield play and dreaming of being able to play there. "When you walked on that field, you knew about the guys that played before you—Tony Bisesi, Ray Mathews, John Butash, Bud Bond—and to be compared with some of those guys and to play on the same field they played on, it was a fabulous feeling."

In some ways, the Rubber Bowl symbolized for years what Akron was all about—blue-collar workers who were proud of their communities and congregated each fall to witness memorable games.

In 1939, construction began on the Rubber Bowl with $516,000 of federal grant money and a $1 subscription drive by area residents. Badges were given to 30,000 Akronites who had given $1 each toward construction. In the first high school game at the stadium on Oct. 11, 1940, Paul Brown's Massillon Tigers defeated Alliance 40-0.

The first game was played a week earlier, Oct. 4, 1940, with Western Reserve University defeating the University of Akron 6-0. The Rubber Bowl is still home of the Zips and is the second-largest college stadium in the state (capacity 35,202).

But over the years, the Rubber Bowl became a "second home" to Akron city teams, too. Akron Mayor Don Plusquellic played at Kenmore in the 1960s, remembering the days when City Series teams scheduled Friday night doubleheaders. "The Rubber Bowl was only 30 years old and it had this mystique to it," said Plusquellic, an All-City quarterback. "I always felt I could throw the ball farther, run faster and play better when I played at the Rubber Bowl under the lights. "I just had the sense that when you played at the Rubber Bowl, no matter who you played, it was a bigger game. Playing there was like becoming a professional player and playing in a professional stadium. It was a major stadium."

Plusquellic and others of that generation knew the Rubber Bowl had been associated with the NFL. The Cleveland Browns played 19 preseason games there (starting in 1946 and ending in 1973 with a few years skipped in between) and a Dallas Texans "home" game was played at the Rubber Bowl on Thanksgiving Day in 1950 after the City Series title game.

"I remember seeing Fran Tarkenton play at the Rubber Bowl against the Browns," Plusquellic said.

The small locker rooms have been remodeled and updated but when Sine and Plusquellic played, they were as simple as could be. They were dark and dank," Sine said. "Not your modern facilities but it was football. You didn't have separations of the offense and defense. You were crowded in there as a team. It was intense. You could hear the people stomping outside. You could smell the popcorn. You could smell the hot dogs. You could hear the band playing and the PA announcer."

Tim Flossie loved the days when he was on the sideline, not as a player or coach, but as a youngster, following around his dad, Babe Flossie, on the sidelines. The games on Thanksgiving Day at the Rubber Bowl brought the entire city together. "I was eight or nine and I'd ride to the Turkey Day game with my mom and the traffic would be backed up from the (Rubber) Bowl all the way to the (Akron airport) circle and up the (Triplett Boulevard) hill," he said. "Turkey Day at the Rubber Bowl was the biggest day of football in Akron. I see some of the guys 30 years later and we still talk about all of those Rubber Bowl stories."

Tim Flossie played for Garfield, then was an assistant coach at East before becoming head coach at Central-Hower and then at Buchtel in the city. Flossie remembers a story about his father's Garfield team facing Kenmore in the 1969 championship game. As Sine recalled, several members of the Garfield team received pacifiers in the mail. They were supposed to have been sent by Kenmore players.

Tim Flossie revealed what really happened. "My dad did that," he said laughing. "I found out years later. He set that whole thing up. He was always doing things like that to get his players fired up."

Bill McGee succeeded Babe Flossie as Rams coach and had many memorable moments among 16 City titles. When the Rams played in the state championship game in 1983, the semifinal game was at the Rubber Bowl and they defeated Mentor Lake Catholic 14-10 in front of more than 15,000.

Former Buchtel star Jay Brophy, now the head football coach at St. Vincent-St. Mary, was a star player for the Griffins in the late 1970s. After high school, Brophy enjoyed a big-time college career at Miami and then played for the Dolphins in the NFL. But he said playing at the Rubber Bowl on Thanksgiving Day is still one of the highlights of his career.

"You woke up smelling turkey cooking in the morning, then you would go to Buchtel before the game for a pancake breakfast," Brophy said. "I was lucky enough to play in three (city) championships and it was the biggest thrill for us back then. It was a dream for us to play on AstroTurf.

"Back then, everybody was so competitive in all the neighborhoods but it was a good thing," Brophy added. "There was a lot of pride between the communities so everybody turned out at the Rubber Bowl to see who was the best and it always seemed to bring the entire city together. It was a beautiful thing."

Former All-City player Charles Parnell had the opportunity to play in a City title game in the early '70s and also had the opportunity to help coach his son (Charles Jr.) and nephew (Renzy Parnell) when the Rams won the title game in 1998 against Buchtel.

"That was a special moment for me," Parnell Sr. said.

Former Kenmore coach Dick Fortner spanned two eras at the Rubber Bowl—grass (or mud) and turf (beginning in 1973). "We went to the wide-open attack and it involved a spread offense with an above-average amount of passing," Fortner said. "And when we had to play at the Rubber Bowl, especially in the playoffs and on Thanksgiving Day, it was always a gamble (with) the risk of having bad weather."

Kenmore wasn't the only school that saw the quality of play sometimes suffer at the Bowl. Because of the number of games played at the facility, the field often grew sloppy as the season progressed. Among City Series teams, Ellet, Buchtel and Kenmore have stadiums that can host a game but Ellet is the only field with lights. Central-Hower, East, Firestone, Garfield and North only have practice fields nearby their school. The City Series solved some scheduling problems with the Friday doubleheaders at the Bowl.

But after AstroTurf was introduced in Houston in 1965 at the Astrodome, the talk grew louder in Akron about making the Rubber Bowl a better place to play. In June 1971, the stadium's management changed hands from the city of Akron to the university. Then in 1973, a gift of $200,000 from Elza E. Hopkins and a local department store chain called Clarkins was added to $160,000 totaled in a fund-raising drive for a new field. The $160,000 amount was coordinated by the Touchdown Club, an Akron all-sports booster group.

Posters around town solicited donations by asking football fans to "get the kids out of the mud." It worked.

Then, in 1983, a second artificial surface was installed to replace the first one. "When they put the turf down, we enjoyed going there even more," Fortner said. Akron Public Schools athletic director Mike Buckner played in three City Series championship games at the Rubber Bowl (1959, '60, '61) while at East and coached in the title game from 1975 to 1978. "Thanksgiving Day was a special morning for families," he said. "Families arranged their dinner around the game and it was a tremendous thing to see 22,000 fans."

Longtime Ellet coach Joe Yost, who lived close by enough to walk to the Rubber Bowl, said he once watched a game that almost couldn't be seen. "When we stood at the intersection of George Washington Boulevard and Triplett, you could hear the voices and you could hear the band, but you could not see the Rubber Bowl, not even the bright lights. Fog rolled into the bowl and filled it up like soup," Yost said. That game was in 1978 and North defeated Garfield 7-0 in a semifinal game of the City Series playoffs.

As a coach, Yost has had two special moments at the Rubber Bowl. One was in 1985, when the Orangemen defeated North 14-6 in a semifinal. "Ellet got to the Thanksgiving Day game for the first time in history and it was something every kid, coach and everyone in the community will never forget." In 1989, Yost coached Ellet to a 7-6 upset of Buchtel, led by star back Ricky Powers, in the title game.

Some people just refuse to let go of traditions. Chuck Shuman is a former East standout quarterback who played in the Thanksgiving city championship games from 1964-66. Shuman currently is an assistant coach at Ellet where his son, Kevin, played quarterback and helped the Orangemen reach that '89 title game.

The last City Series Thanksgiving Day championship game was in 1990, as an announced crowd of about 4,000 sat in the rain and watched Buchtel rally to defeat Garfield 26-22.

"I probably shouldn't admit this," Chuck Shuman said, "but ever since they stopped playing the Turkey Day game, my son Kevin and I sneak into the Rubber Bowl every Thanksgiving Day and throw the football around for 15 minutes or a half-hour. We just throw the ball, talk and reminisce. That's how much that game and that stadium means to us."

Here's how former players, coaches and fans recalled their favorite memories from "The Bowl."

Joe Yost, Ellet coach, Summit County Sports Hall of Famer and the longest tenured coach in the league, in his 29th season: "In 1985, we played North in a playoff game. The week before North beat us 20-0 in the last game of the season. We had two weeks to get ready for them in the playoffs, and we were going to wear our orange.

"Just before that game, we went back in the locker room for our team prayer. I mentioned to the kids that it was going to be a dark night and that a black cloud would be coming over the bowl, then I pulled out a black jersey. The Peewee organization bought us all black jerseys to wear just for that game, and I passed them all out to our guys and we went on to win that game. Garfield beat us in the championship, but it was the first time in our school history that we had ever been to the championship game. It was still such a great night for the kids. And they were allowed to keep those black jerseys they wore against North. The biggest personal memory I have of the Rubber Bowl is the first time I saw my brother Gary on a kickoff while playing for Akron. He was cut his first year; the second year he walked on. He later became a special-teams player, then became a starting defensive back and captain. Not bad for a guy who started out at 155 pounds and worked himself to 215 pounds. I knew how hard he worked, and I was very proud of him."

Former Garfield coach Bill McGee: "One of my favorite memories is when we played Mentor Lake Catholic in the state semifinal in 1983 and beat them 14-10 in front of a crowd of about 15,000 or 16,000.

"But all of my favorite memories of the Rubber Bowl are all the (City) championship games we won. The championship we won in 2001 was special because it was my last year as head coach. We beat Buchtel (7-6) and not a lot of teams beat Buchtel back then."

Mike Buckner, former City football coach and former City Series athletic director; Buckner's association with the City Series and the Rubber Bowl dates to the late 1950s. He starred at East, graduating in 1962, and later played at Northwestern; he had several family members play in the City Series, including his three sons, Michael, Brandon and Tobin: "As a player, we lost three years to Garfield at the Bowl and I'd say that my sophomore and senior years we were a better team, man to man. But my junior year, Ray Mathews ran for three touchdowns for Garfield that game and that hurt us the most." Years later, Buckner got some gratification, as Buchtel coach. "In 1975, that was the first year we made the (City) playoffs. . . . We upset Garfield . . . that was a great game for us."

Mike Ede, St. Vincent-St. Mary, Class of 1975, two-time first-team All-*Beacon Journal* linebacker (1974-75): "My most memorable moment was when we played Hoban and I'm pretty sure it was in '75. Hoban was driving on us and it was third and long. We broke the huddle and I was in my stance. Then all of a sudden, I heard a voice behind me say, 'Hey Ede, watch the draw. Watch the draw, Ede.'

"The voice wasn't familiar, so I knew it wasn't one of my teammates. When I turned around, it was the referee telling me to watch for the draw. I couldn't believe it. Well, the play wasn't a draw anyway, so the crybabies at Hoban can't say I knew the play. Plus, we won the game. That's all that matters."

Tim Flossie, longtime City Series football coach who won back-to-back state championships at Buchtel (1987-88); son of the late Garfield coach Babe Flossie: "I went from a water boy to a player to a coach, so there are so many memories for me. As a kid, I remember going to the games on Thanksgiving Day and the traffic was so bad, it would be backed up all the way up the hill to Thomastown School and it would take you an hour to get to the Bowl. And once you got inside, there were almost 20,000 people from all over the city there.

"As a coach, one of my best memories is when I was coaching at Buchtel and we played Garfield in the last Thanksgiving Day game there. That was really special."

Michelle Marquess-Kearns, principal at Litchfield Middle School and former softball and volleyball standout at North; her father, Charles Marquess, was a football coach at North: "My favorite memories of the Rubber Bowl were the Friday night doubleheaders. My dad was the head coach at North, so it felt like we always spent Friday night at the Rubber Bowl. More than anything, those games really showed an incredible sense of community pride and spirit because every week, the fans would fill the Rubber Bowl."

Jerry Laria, longtime City Series basketball coach at Garfield and Firestone: "For me, it was a playoff game in the early '80s. I was an assistant coach under Dave Marshall. There had to be at least 6 inches of snow on the ground. The wind and snow was blowing so hard, the lights inside the stadium were rocking back and forth. There were probably only about 25 people left in the stadium, and those people had to be crazy.

"When we left, we watched a little bit of the second game between North and Ellet and it took us an hour to get back home. Before the game, I told coach Marshall that we should kick off first because they would probably fumble at some point because of the conditions. Two plays after the kickoff, they did fumble and a few plays later, we scored, and I think that was the only score of the game."

Trenton Lykes, Firestone quarterback and Youngstown State hall of famer; Lykes played for Jim Tressel in the mid-'80s and Tressel said Lykes was responsible for putting YSU's program on the national map in the '90s; Lykes has a unique perspective because, although he had big games in the Rubber Bowl with the Falcons, his biggest moment came when he returned to the Rubber Bowl as a YSU senior: "My most memorable game was the last game I played there, which was November of '87.

"What truly made the game memorable was the playing conditions, because a blizzard hit the area. The first half was cold and snowy, but the second half was so bad that when I went under center, I had to turn my head left or right to call the plays because the snow was blowing so hard. I could not see nor talk if I kept my mouth open for too long. We couldn't even watch film of the game because the film was just all white. I don't remember the score of the game but I do know it was close. . . . It was one of those games that was really fun, if you won."

AUTHOR'S INSPIRATION

As a member of the media, I HATED the Rubber Bowl. As a fan, however, I loved it because my first-ever experience with the "Bowl" was in 1974, when my dad took me there to watch my alma mater, Warren G. Harding, beat Cincinnati Moeller for the Class AAA (Division I) state championship.

Years later, as a professional journalist, I *still* hated the Rubber Bowl, because it was just old and outdated. But it wasn't until I was hired at the *Akron Beacon Journal*, after I moved to Akron from Youngstown, after I immersed myself in the Akron community, that I realized how special the Rubber Bowl really was to those in the area.

I started to understand that they called it "The Bowl." That's all Akronites needed to say when they talked about watching memorable football games at the Rubber Bowl.

Turkey Day games always seemed to be accompanied by blizzard conditions and 10 inches of snow.

No matter how terrible the weather, players and fans knew that waiting at home was a fantastic Thanksgiving dinner sure to warm the body and soul. The dinner table was where they could replay the highlights of the game with family and friends.

In the fall of 2009, the University of Akron began play in the new 33,000-seat Infocision Stadium. But I have to admit, I'm very proud to have had the opportunity to work at the Bowl.

AFTERWORD

The truth with Northeast Ohio high school sports is that it's a wonderful spectacle that starts with the football season. And how exciting is the start of the football season?

It's no surprise to see plenty of cameras on the scene at a high school football game. There are parents taking Kodak moment pictures, others shooting video with hand-held minicams. There are coaches with cameras mounted on tripods recording the entire game for scouting, grading and record-keeping. And, oh yes, for a few lucky schools each Friday night, there's the invasion of WJW's SkyFox television camera crew, complete with its wildly popular, noisy helicopter landing nearby.

"SkyFox" is the nickname for the helicopter used by WJW (Channel 8) for news coverage that includes as many high school football games as they can get to on a Friday night. SkyFox has a powerful gyroscopic camera called the Ultra Media III. It can zoom in on an object from up to a mile and a half away.

The station's reporters and videographers can watch the action, scan the crowd and swoop in on the scoreboard without even being near the stadium. Videographer Bob Wilkinson said: "There's no better way to cover high school football than this. And the best part is, you never have to worry about parking."

I was covering a football game at Copley one Friday evening when I heard a commotion in the stands. Everyone was looking toward the sky and waving. When I peered my head out of the pressbox, I saw what everyone else saw. It was Fox 8's SkyFox helicopter just about to land adjacent to the stadium, in an open area.

It was really neat seeing this huge helicopter landing so close. SkyFox and the other Cleveland television stations routinely use their company helicopters to enhance their Friday night high school football coverage. Just then, the thought occurred to me—I should arrange to fly with one of the television stations on a Friday.

The idea was a hit with my editor and Fox 8 allowed me to accompany them and it was an awesome experience.

On the opening week of the season, Lake High was playing at Copley when Fox 8 sports anchor Tony Rizzo and a camera operator emerged from the aircraft amid cheers and applause.

There's something about the arrival of the helicopter that gets a crowd excited. It was as if Rizzo was a rock star as fans flocked toward him just for the chance to say hello. Besides Rizzo, the SkyFox crew includes sports reporter Dan Coughlin, Wilkinson and pilot Bob Koenig during their Friday night coverage.

Fox 8's weekly Friday adventure begins around 3 P.M., because that's when Senate League high school games are played in Cleveland. On a recent Friday, coverage started at a game between East Tech and Glenville that Glenville easily won.

Coughlin is well-known by sports fans for being on television, but he previously worked for newspapers, too. "Hey, Dan. You're the man," a fan said at the East Tech-Glenville game.

"Hey, great to see you, too," Coughlin answered back.

Coughlin's reputation for being outgoing and friendly makes him perfect for the Friday night assignments. He can strike up a casual conversation with a head coach such as East Tech's Gerald Stueber while the game is in progress.

Coughlin's videographer is Dave Bradford. The idea in covering the daytime games is to get as many highlights as they can to "make it look like we've been there the whole game," Coughlin said.

Bradford added, "After doing this for so long, you start to anticipate what's going to happen on the field and you're able to get the shots you need." On the way to catch the next Senate League game, Coughlin, sitting in the front seat, turned to a passenger in the back seat and said, "Are you hungry?"

The response: "Um, a little bit."

Coughlin: "Well, you should have packed a lunch."

Coughlin and Bradford both started laughing.

While at Rhodes, a *Beacon Journal* photographer suffered a slight injury, cutting his finger on a fence. "In this game, you learn to play with pain," Coughlin said. A week ago, because the Indians were playing a home game in the middle of a pennant race, Rizzo was assigned to report at Jacobs Field.

So Coughlin was on the football beat as SkyFox came from Burke Lakefront Airport in Cleveland and touched down at Green Memorial Stadium with 6:26 left in the first quarter. As usual, fans of all ages gathered along the fence to greet the helicopter. Coughlin waved to the crowd, then made his way to the field, along with Wilkinson and Koenig.

"I've flown for news with other stations but this, by far, is my favorite thing to do," said Koenig, who has been flying for Fox 8 the past five years. "We're the only ones who go all out for high school football. We're the only ones this hardcore."

Koenig prepares for the hectic night by calling school athletic directors Tuesday and Wednesday to alert them that SkyFox would like to land briefly near their stadium. "They are always really excited about it," Koenig said. "We talk about places where I can land, a soccer field or practice field next to the stadium, where there's no power lines or anything like that."

Once they land, Coughlin and Wilkinson dash up and down the sideline to get their video, then they all signal each other and it's time to move on to the next game. The next destination was Perry High in Massillon for the Panthers' home game against Canton McKinley. It took just nine minutes to fly from Green to Perry Stadium at 110 mph.

The scene was the same at Perry. SkyFox landed, people started to cheer and Coughlin did the star routine all over again. Just before takeoff from Perry en route to the Louisville-Canton South game, Koenig noticed a man with two dogs on a leash outside the stadium. Koenig said, "Look at those nice dogs."

Coughlin replied, "They're probably 'Air'dales."

After arriving at Canton South, Coughlin worked the sidelines and took careful note of the time. It was around 9:30 p.m., and SkyFox had to be back in Cleveland by 10:10 or 10:15 at the latest so the videotape could be edited and ready for the sports news segment of the hour news report, starting at approximately 10:40. Heading out of Stark County, the stadium lights from other schools were visible.

"There's North Canton," someone said. A few minutes later, someone said, "There's Green again." Locations were noted along the way for most of the flight back to Cleveland.

"There's Springfield."

"There's the Rubber Bowl."

"There's Mogadore."

"There's Tallmadge."

From the air, it was easy to distinguish the Chapel Hill Mall area below and then state Route 8, continuing over Interstate 271 and the Ohio Turnpike. Ahead in the distance, tops of large buildings came into view. Of course, it was Cleveland.

Wilkinson grabbed the control panel that maneuvers the camera outside the helicopter and zoomed in on Jacobs Field. He was able to get the stadium lights in view and the script "Indians" sign was visible at the top of the stadium.

When SkyFox landed back at Burke Lakefront at about 10:04 P.M., Coughlin and Wilkinson grabbed their equipment and raced to their car. Wilkinson drove along North Marginal Road, crossed over I-90 and pulled into the Fox 8 parking lot, just a few minutes from the airport. Inside the station, Coughlin handed off the tapes to sports producer Dan Jovic.

"Some of these news people complain about working Election Night," Coughlin said, as he raced through the hallway. "Every Friday night is like Election Night for us." As editors worked on making the final tape, Coughlin wrote a script to match the highlights.

Co-anchor John Telich also was writing his script. Telich was covering games that evening by car while Rizzo was at his desk, watching the Indians battle the Chicago White Sox in what ended up being a 13-inning loss.

As expected, Coughlin and the rest of the sports team made their deadline.

The sports portion of the broadcast began, and Coughlin went smoothly on the air live in the studio. Between, Rizzo, Coughlin and Telich, the sports segment was its usual entertaining show with lots of scores and highlights.

"When we get on air, it's the fastest seven minutes in television," Coughlin said. "This is what makes it all worthwhile. You can't beat this feeling and I love doing it."

APPENDIX

Stories by Year of Publication

2009

Boy Tosses Aside Early Limitations, June 14

2008

Dream Becomes Tall Order, February 14
Tallmadge Family Bands Together, February 21
"Superstar" Song Motivates Athletes, April 17
Putting Value of Education First, Foremost, April 27
Diversity, Golf Meet Every Young Golfer, June 20
LeBron Emotional at Movie Premiere, September 9
School Tragedy Illustrates Fragility of Life, October 10
Akron Girl's Hard Work Wins Over Neighborhood, October 16
A Warrior of All Seasons, November 13

2007

East Lineman Dies at Akron Hospital, January 3
Giving Up Not Option to Dedicated Revere Boys, January 25
Swimmer Dives into Life After Team, February 1
Central-Hower's Coach Moves to N.C., February 15
St. V-M Golfer to Play for His Grandpa, October 11
Players Pass It Forward, December 20

2006

Woodridge Junior Scoring Off Court, January 19
All Players Have Shot to Live Dream, January 23
Athletes Are Role Models, April 11
Hudson Wins Team Title, May 20
Franek Is Absolutely Fantastic, June 4
On Stage or In Stadium, Athleticism Counts, June 12
Family Affair, Sisters Raise St. V-M Football Player, November 16
Wrestling Just Like Family, December 14
CYO Coach Training Helps Protect Kids, December 14

2005

Umping the Ante, July 10
Bad Actions Forever Alter Young Lives, October 27

2004

Parker Slam Dunks Basketball, Myths, April 3
Area Youth Leader Dies at Age of 70, May 4
Athlete Clears Hurdle to Succeed, May 11
Girl Becomes Gridiron Star, October 6
Family Matters, October 8

2003

Irish Star Keeps It in Perspective, January 22
52-Pick Up for LeBron, February 9
St. V-M Nearly Reaches Summit, February 16
A Little Bit of Baseball, a Big Dose of Salvation, June 18
In Her Own Class, Good Model for Student-Athletes, June 29
Traveling Fan's Soccer Team, September 2

2002

Oak Hill Wins War: James Shines, February 11
Cover Boy Is All Smiles, February 14

Buchtel High Coach Dies During Surgery, February 27
James Is Handling Flood Well, March 23
Three Was Just Not to Be, March 24
Love of the Game Overcomes Adversity, April 23
Baseball Player Steps Up in Crisis, April 24
Hec(tor) of a Good Time, June 11
The Tausch Family Always Enjoys Hosting Aeros Players, July 10
'The Bowl' Games Bowl 'Em Over, August 19
Reputation Precedes Garfield's Boys Coach, September 24
Buchtel's Jones Is One of the Boys, October 2
Tears Flow for Athlete, October 12
Vitale Gets Chance to See James, November 27

2001

St. V-M Nearly Reaches Summit, January 14
St. V-M: Things You Didn't Know, March 19
This Little Guy's a Big Shot, March 24
Mikenna Racing the Long Run, May 24
Stringer Played Big on Field, August 7

2000

White Delivers Christian Message, February 18
Invincible Irish, March 26
Buchtel High, Yale Mold the Lives of Two Teammates, November 13
From Backboards to Blackboards, December 24

1999

The Heart of the Matter, August 27
Ellet Quarterback Leffler Gets Call, September 2

1996

A Family Affair, Jackson Football, October 8